The Classic Italian Garden

The Classic Italian Garden

JUDITH CHATFIELD

Photographs by
LIBERTO PERUGI

RIZZOLI
NEW YORK

Horticulture
Indianapolis Museum

A two-part series:
The Classic Italian Garden
A Tour of Italian Gardens

First published in the United States of America in 1991 by
Rizzoli International Publications, Inc.
300 Park Avenue South
New York, New York 10010

Library of Congress Cataloging-in-Publication Data
Chatfield, Judith.
The classic Italian garden / Judith Chatfield; photographs by
Liberto Perugi.
p. cm.
ISBN 0-8478-1398-3
1. Gardens, Italian—History. 2. Gardens—Italy—History. 3. Gardens, Italian—Picto-
rial works. 4. Gardens—Italy—Pictorial works. I. Title.
SB457.85.C36 1991
712'.0945—dc20

Typeset by Graphic Composition, Inc., Athens, Georgia
Printed and bound in Hong Kong
Design by Mary McBride
Copyediting by Jean Quayle
Jacket illustration: Villa Agape, Florence
Title page: Castello di Uzzano, Greve in Chianti

Contents

Introduction

Italy over the centuries has produced an astonishing artistic output, unmatched by any other country. The Italian imagination, flair for design, and craftsmanship extend into every facet of life. Hence, it should be no surprise that Italy is a land of remarkable gardens. The Italian garden, like Italian literature, is not coldly rational, but very human and individualistic. Each garden has its personalized charm and touch of the unexpected. They have delighted foreign travelers over the ages—their descriptions appearing in journals and letters, and their concepts exported abroad to shape transalpine gardens.

One hundred years ago the Classic Italian garden became an object of study for English and American writers. Charles A. Platt published his photographs in 1896, followed by C. Latham in 1905. Edith Wharton was sent to Italy to do a series of garden articles which were later illustrated by Maxfield Parrish and published as a book in 1905, the same year that Latham's photographs came out. The next year, H. Inigo Triggs published architectural plans of the gardens. Luigi Dami's collection of photographs and old engravings came out in an English edition in 1924, followed by the Renaissance garden plans of J. C. Shepherd and G. A. Jellicoe. During the 1930s the English landscape architect Cecil Pinsent went to Italy, where he created a number of Renaissance-inspired gardens, including I Tatti in Florence and Villa la Foce in the Val d'Orcia. In 1961 Georgina Masson wrote her study of Italian gardens, which is still unsurpassed. Currently there is a revival of interest in the history of gardens, particularly Italian gardens. Several universities in the United States offer courses in garden and landscape history. At the University of Florence the architectural faculty is experimenting with a course on garden preservation and restoration.

There still remain serious research lacunas in the far northern reaches of Italy and south of Naples. Surviving formal gardens are few in these regions. Perhaps this is attributable to harsh extremes of climate and terrain, and to economic factors which did not favor the creation or upkeep of such gardens. Maintenance costs are staggering, and many a formal garden has been revamped in English landscape style for ease of upkeep—or simply abandoned. In Sicily, the Moorish gardens of Palermo have vanished, and later formal gardens were transformed into landscape parks. Little remains in Sicily apart from the Medieval cloister garden of Monreale and the Baroque whimsy of Bagheria, today reduced to a bare courtyard with grotesque statues topping its walls.

The previously mentioned authors provided a framework to search out surviving gardens designed in the Classic Italian style. The major gardens—apart from a few that were inaccessible at the time or in phases of restoration, such as Villa Litta at Lainate—were published in my first volume, *A Tour of Italian Gardens*, in 1988. Some of these proved to be in a very fragmentary condition, yet were included because of their historical importance. The Classic gardens of Genoa are extremely fragmentary. The fabled Este and Gonzaga gardens of Ferrara and Mantua have vanished, and many of the Savoy gardens surrounding Turin are in lamentable condition. By contrast, the Medici gardens of Florence and the gardens of princes and cardinals in and around Rome have survived almost intact. Gardens in the north have often undergone transformation because the flatter terrain was easier to convert into English landscape parks, whereas the more rugged terrain of Tuscany and the hills of Rome ensured the survival of terraces and staircases. Also, the north was subject by proximity to French fashions of the eighteenth century. Their parterres are apt to be in *broderie*, or flowing designs resembling embroidery, rather than geometric patterns. These northern gardens tend to emphasize the horizontal layout, changing vistas at different viewpoints. Yet the French garden is basically an outgrowth of the Italian garden, so elements of the Classic garden remain.

These Italian elements include a strong symmetrical axial design, with interpenetration of villa and garden. In Tuscany the gardens are predominantly defined by evergreen material, in Rome by architectural use of stone, where vegetation is secondary. Water flowing through channels, fountains, and *nymphaeums* (grottoes dedicated to the nymphs) is important in the hot Italian climate. During the Renaissance, gardens first flourished in Tuscany—cradle of the humanist movement. Ancient Roman texts such as Varro and Pliny were reread, inspiring a love for country villa life. Leon Battista Alberti's influential *De re aedificatoria* of 1452 described the ideal garden: one that takes into consideration site and includes pergolas, lawns, clipped hedges, topiary—shaped trees or hedges—spelling out the owner's name, grottoes, and a summerhouse. This was a geometric, evergreen garden. Francesco Colonna's allegorical romance *Hypnerotomachia Poliphili* was written in 1467, and later published with woodcuts depicting garden pavilions and fountains, which served as models for garden patrons. Gardens were designed with geometrical parterres, pergolas, labyrinths, fountains, and grottoes—some wonderfully fantastic ones such as Bernardo Buontalenti's and il Tribolo's creations at Pratolino, Boboli, and Castello. Beyond them were orchards and game preserves. Early in the sixteenth century, Donato Bramante terraced the garden courtyard of the Vatican Belvedere, setting the mode for architectural gardens. This style of terracing was further developed by Raphael and the Sangallos at Villa Madama, which incorporated surrounding views from the terraced hillside. Staircases and water cascades became more and more elaborate as the Baroque garden developed. Definition became blurred, lines softened, and the ever-vaster garden dissolved in the distance into the *bosco*— a shady grove of trees implying a wilderness.

In this volume I have attempted to trace the predecessors of the Classic Italian garden in chapters on ancient Roman gardens (focusing on Pompeii and Hadrian's Villa); Medieval cloister gardens; and enclosed, courtly Renaissance gardens. Chapters on two early surviving botanical gardens in Pisa and Padua are included in the interest of historical thoroughness, rather than the development of garden design. A few gardens designed in the 1930s have been included for their spirit of revival of the Classic garden. Although I have avoided selecting landscape park gardens, a number of the gardens here are partially such. They were chosen, however, for the formal elements that still conform to the Classic garden; yet for the traveler on the spot, the park sections are described. Many of the problems Edith Wharton encountered in researching gardens remain today. The gardens are usually located out of town and not easily tracked down. Property owners change, as do the names of the villas. Most proprietors have generously opened their garden gates for this book, sharing their pride in their gardens. A few were reluctant, not wishing to display the extent of neglect the gardens had suffered.

There is a need to document these fragile works of art before they vanish. Many, fortunately, are now protected by Italian law; being registered prohibits radical alterations, but does not ensure their upkeep. Public interest is growing and the demand to visit private gardens is increasing. The Fondo Ambiente Italiano (FAI) is attempting to preserve properties in Italy, opening them to the public. But the vast majority of gardens are still in private hands and without government support for their costly maintenance. These gardens are symbols of continuity and recall the generations of families who maintained and embellished them over the years. Gardens are living, breathing creations, unique among art works, touching the imagination of all who enter them.

Ancient Roman Gardens

Gardens of Pompeii and Tivoli are open to the public; ask guardians to open locked areas

The Canopus at Hadrian's Villa, Tivoli

The ancient Roman Republic extolled as a virtue the citizen working his land. We have only to recall the example of Cincinnatus, a model Roman patriot who was found tending his farm during a revolt in the city in 458 B.C.; at the behest of the Senate, he assumed dictatorship, saved Rome from the Aequi, then stepped down from power to return to his beloved farm. Around the first century B.C., as slave labor gradually became the norm, this ideal was pushed aside.

The first Roman gardens were simple ones—producing fruit and vegetables, with only a few flowers to adorn family altars and tombs. The roots of the Classic Italian gardens can be traced back to the first century B.C., after Sulla's conquest of Athens. The returning Roman soldiers brought home impressions of the late Hellenistic gardens and the *paradeisoi*—the lush hunting parks of the Persians. There were Assyrian and Egyptian influences as well that filtered into the Romans' new enthusiasm for gardens. Two types of garden slowly evolved during the empire. The first was intimately linked with the house; surviving examples of this are still visible at Pompeii. The second was conceived of more loosely as a landscape park. The idea of "villa" in the late empire encompassed a group of buildings linked by allées, porticoes, steps, and passageways; the overall landscaping played a major part in the total concept, with more formal gardens located within the buildings. Hadrian's Villa at Tivoli is the prime survivor of this type of garden.

Besides excavations, our sources of knowledge about the early Roman gardens are based on paintings and literary texts. Wall frescoes were often used to extend the perspective in a garden, and therefore depicted gardens showing plants, fountains, trelliswork, thick bosquets, and often fruit trees. Varro, the first century B.C. Roman scholar, describes in *De re rustica* his elaborate aviary and fishpond complex. But the most complete written descriptions of Roman gardens appear in the letters of Pliny the Younger to his friend Apollinaris. These detailed accounts of his own villas throughout Italy stress their sites, which were carefully chosen for views and healthful breezes. (In Renaissance times Leon Battista Alberti would advise just such hillside sites for the ideal villa.) Pliny describes multiple

areas for specific outdoor activities such as walking, dining, riding, and resting.

The shaping of plant material, such as box and cypress—or topiary—became an art in Roman times. A *topiarius* did the work, creating forms often with mythological or historical themes; hence, scenes such as the destruction of the Niobids or the hunt of the Calydonian boar might be depicted in the villa park.

In all gardens—large and small—the element of water was highly important. Roman aqueducts and advanced hydraulics ensured abundant supplies. It was commonplace to find fountains, canals, and trickling grottoes in Roman gardens. Springs were thought to be sacred to nymphs, an idea which was revived in the sixteenth century in the *nymphaeum* (a grotto dedicated to nymphs) of Villa Giulia. A text by Erone on hydraulics was much studied in the Renaissance for its information on water pressure applied to automata and water organs. Without knowledge of this text, the fabulous grottoes of Pratolino, above Florence, would not have existed.

Ninety-three varieties of plants have been identified at Pompeii by making casts of the calcified roots buried under volcanic ash in household gardens. Although certain species no longer exist, the gardens can be recreated with boxwood, roses, violets, Florentine blue irises, and hyacinths. Maritime pines, pomegranates, planes, poplars, cypresses, and firs were all in existence in A.D. 79 when the city was destroyed.

Unlike the Greeks who considered their homes as mere shelter, Roman homes were sacred. Originally, the house consisted of an atrium, with an opening in its roof for light. Rainwater collected in a shallow small pool (*impluvium*) in the center. With time the private living activity of the family shifted further back in the house to the peristyle, and the atrium was reserved for public visits. The peristyle was a raised, four-sided walkway with columns facing the open center. The center was a *viridarium*, filled with plants, usually having a fountain or pool, and decorated with sculpture and frescoes under the portico. The dining room (*triclinium*) usually faced this peristyle, and sometimes looked beyond to open gardens reaching to the edge of the property. The open gardens could contain trellised walkways along canals, fruit trees, and flowerbeds. Usually a small altar, or *aedicula*, to the household gods was located in this far garden. Some fountains were quite elaborate with steps for the water to course down, set with mosaics and shells (symbol of Venus and fertility). Statues of animals and Dionysiac or fertility gods were often present.

Pompeii is lovely on a late spring afternoon. The golden light bathes the ruins and gives them life. An abundance of wildflowers and green vegetation softens the appearance of so much stone. At such a time it is easy to recreate in the mind's eye the gardens of the private houses. Pompeii was a resort and trading town at the base of Mount Vesuvius, which erupted in A.D. 79, covering the city with ash

The atrium of Villa Cinghiale, with its impluvium *at the back*

for centuries. The taste of the gardens and their art work tended to be more middle class than that of nearby Herculaneum (statues found in Pompeii are apt to be contemporary Roman decorative creations, whereas in Herculaneum they are often copies of Hellenistic works). The elaborate Villa dei Papiri and its garden, excavated in Herculaneum in the eighteenth century, has been recreated as the J. Paul Getty Museum in California. Gardens in Herculaneum were often sited on the hillside to take advantage of the sea views, and as such, were treated as an intermediary stage between house and the water.

The Villa dei Vettii is one of the best-preserved larger houses in Pompeii. One enters through the atrium with its *impluvium*. Across the dark corridor is the sunny peristyle. The dining room is placed at its far end and enjoys the view of its entire length. The walls of the peristyle are frescoed with garden motifs. Within is a large garden with fourteen fountains, their lead piping and valves still functional. The abundance of water and fountains in Pompeiian gardens dates from the construction of the Augustan aqueduct between 28 B.C. and A.D. 14. Originally, the garden was planted with laurel, pomegranate, oleanders, roses, violets, hyacinths, lilies, acanthus, and ivy. Today, bergenia, primroses, roses, daisies, and pansies grow there. Between the columns are marble and bronze sculptures. This Pompeiian building was restructured by two wealthy businessmen soon before the destruction of the city. The Villa of Loreius Tiburtinus contains the largest Pompeiian garden, with a great variety of architectural elements. Its garden is reached through a small peristyle and a long loggia. Beneath it is a large, walled sunken garden. From the loggia a waterfall feeds a parallel canal broken by a temple at its

The peristyle of Villa Giulia Felix

A garden fresco at the House of Venus

middle. Water flows from its *nymphaeum* into a second canal that courses the length of the garden. This is known as an *euripus* (a series of communicating basins), and it is a typical feature of Pompeiian gardens. Another is found in the garden of Giulia Felix, where the second canal is interrupted by a basin and another temple. Wooden pergolas flank the canal. Additional shade was provided by large trees around the confining walls of the garden.

These Pompeiian gardens are designed axially, a canon which will be taken up again in the Renaissance. In the garden is a *biclinium*, a pool with seats around the edge, and a table in the center rising up from the water. Plaster casts have been made of plant roots found in this garden, and once again, figs, chestnuts, pomegranates, and pears flourish in the garden.

The Casa del Fauno Danzante, or House of the Dancing Faun, has a small column-shaped well in its box-edged garden. Red roses bloom and in the rear garden beyond are oleanders and cypress, as well as a palm. Palm trees were only grown in city gardens at this time.

A freestanding, blue mosaic niche stands in the garden of the Casa degli Scienziati or House of the Scientists. A similar one, bordered with scallops and small conch shells, was found in the garden of Marcus Lucretius. Here within the niche, water flowed from a marble statue of the Dionysiac figure of Silenus, companion to Bacchus, down marble steps into a canal with another fountain. Statuettes of animals graced this garden.

The House of Venus has box-bordered beds in its peristyle, with a fresco of Venus reclining on a seashell at the far end under a portico. Nearby, the Villa Giulia Felix functioned as a hotel and has a large garden beyond the confines of the house itself. A long, marble-edged *euripus* is spanned by small bridges. Bordering it is a long portico with grottoes and altars. The garden also included a vegetable garden and orchard to provide fruit for the conclusion of meals, an expected mark of hospitality.

Hadrian's Villa at Tivoli is a grandiose assembly of buildings fit for an emperor. They appear to have been placed randomly into the hollow above the gorge and falls of Tivoli. Much of the villa's drama stems from the surrounding countryside, which has been compared to the Vale of Tempe in Greece, for the wild plunge of the gorge, the gentler undulating terrain where the buildings are set, the Tibertine hills to the north, and the vast sweep of the Roman countryside in

Strada dell'Abbondanza—the ruins of partially excavated shops overgrown with poppies and yellow broom plants

The euripus *of Villa Giulia Felix*

the distance to the south. The combination of the extensive country-side outside the villa buildings and the intimate gardens within are characteristic of Roman gardens of the empire period.

The scale is overwhelming, but was deemed necessary in its day to impress and accommodate the enormous entourage of courtiers and staff. Construction began the year after Hadrian became emperor, in A.D. 118, ceasing with his death in A.D. 138. The Barbarian invaders in the ensuing centuries were so awed by it that they left it alone. For years it was abandoned. During Medieval times it became a huge quarry, its marble and stone carted off to build the nearby town of Tivoli. Further spoilation ensued in the Renaissance when its sculptures, mosaics, and ornaments were removed to the Vatican. During that period the architect Pirro Ligorio came to the site and carefully recorded what remained. Between 1550 and 1560, he was employed by Cardinal d'Este to design the spectacular Villa d'Este and its gardens. Details of that garden and others in the Renaissance found their source here.

Unlike Pompeii, the gardens have not been replanted with flowers, but in spring the scent of lilacs, the sound of water rippling across the large pools, the birds, and the sight of wildflowers evokes the gardens' glorious past.

Looking at the scale model at the entrance, it is evident that the buildings are built on a strictly axial basis. Much visited by Renaissance garden architects, Hadrian's Villa left its imprint on sixteenth-century garden design, linking house and garden intimately with a strong central axis. The unifying use of water, too, was not overlooked in the Renaissance. Spread out over more than seven hundred acres, the buildings were connected by *viales*—broad avenues, porticoes, and steps. The vast, unified plan of Hadrian's Villa became a model for Roman seventeenth-century gardens.

The much-traveled emperor recreated at Tivoli monuments and sites, albeit not to scale, of places he had visited. The result is a museum-garden, intended to evoke distant places, and to provide a setting for his fabulous art collection, especially in the Piazza d'Oro, with its large open courtyards, once adorned with sculpture. An atrium opened onto the southern wall, leading to a curved *nymphaeum.*

Its mammoth Pecile, a gymnasium with covered walkways around an open rectangular pool, was thought to have been inspired by the Stoa Poikile in Athens. The northern wall had a portico on either side, enabling the stroller to choose between shade or sun.

Highly intriguing is the Marine Theater, which was probably intended for private dining or study, although its exact use is uncertain. Within walls is a portico of Ionic columns encircling an elliptical canal faced in marble. An oval island with a retractable bridge had a small pavilion surrounding a tiny central garden with a fountain. The bridge seen today is permanent, put in place when the Marine

Villa dei Vettii, a patrician villa with its recreated peristyle garden. A sophisticated hydraulic system supplied fourteen fountains

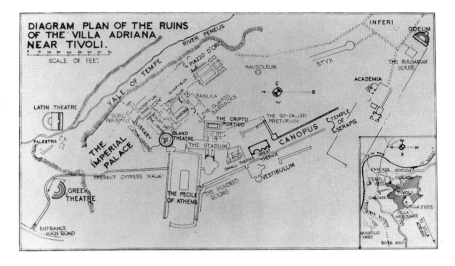

Theater was restored in 1955.

Most evocative is the Canopus, named after the easternmost delta of the Nile. The Nile is represented by the canal, cradled by a wildflower-covered bank and the ruins of the temple of Serapis, the Egyptian god of fertility. This temple in Egypt was a place of pilgrimage to consult an oracle. It has been suggested that Hadrian's lover, young Antinous, may have died after the oracle predicted a long life for the emperor if a young man died for him. Be that as it may, Antinous died mysteriously in Egypt. In the past the emperor's collection of Egyptian sculpture lined the sides of the canal. There is still a marble crocodile remaining; the other statues are now found in the Vatican museums. Copies of the caryatids on the Erectheum of the Athens Acropolis stand midway along the canal supporting the roof of a loggia. The opposite side of the canal was bordered by a colonnade acting as a shady pergola. The northern end of the canal is marked by a semicircular *triclinium* (or dining area) with views of the countryside. Swans still swim today in the green waters.

Above the gorge stand the remaining four columns of the circular Temple of Venus, the prototype for that most popular of eighteenth-century romantic garden pavilions.

The Italian state acquired the property in 1870 and at last halted the pilfering of the site. (The first systematic search for treasure began under Pope Alexander VI in the late fifteenth century and continued under Cardinal Alessandro Farnese, who hauled away many statues to the Orti Farnesiani as mayor of Tivoli in 1533; it was then further plundered by Cardinal Ippolito d'Este between 1550 and 1572). Serious restoration work commenced after World War II.

Cloister Gardens

Cloister gardens are open to the public:

Santi Quattro Coronati, Rome
San Francesco, Fiesole
San Damiano, Assisi
Certosa, Galluzzo (Florence)
Certosa, Pavia
Sant'Uffizio, Cioccaro di Penango

Gardens played a significant part in the teachings of the early Church fathers. In the beginning of the fifth century, at Hippo on the African coast, Saint Augustine was given a garden in which he could discuss his religious ideas, continuing the tradition of Greek scholars in Athens who met outdoors in gardens. Around the same time, Saint Jerome, who had settled in a monastery in Bethlehem, urged his followers to hoe the ground, plant cabbages, and irrigate them.

Gardens in the first monasteries were not planted for their aesthetic or symbolic qualities; they were strictly utilitarian, providing food and medicine. Around the year 1000, the idea of a garden as an ideal microcosm, perfection of the wilderness beyond the monastic walls, evolved as the *hortus conclusus* (enclosed garden). In Medieval times the importance of the Virgin Mary was elevated into a cult reflected even in gardens; hence the enclosed garden symbolized the womb of the Virgin Mary. It was also interpreted as representing the Garden of Eden. The garden became the antithesis of the *selva*—the wild forest, a symbol of the soul separated from the untamed world— here cared for and cultivated by the grace of God within protecting walls.

Ecclesiastical cloister gardens are direct descendents of the ancient Roman peristyle gardens. The early Christian hermits often settled in the ruins of Roman country villas. In 494 Saint Benedict did so at Subiaco, planting a rose garden amid the ruined walls. Later, when he moved to Cassino, he again lived in an old Roman villa. When he founded his order around 530 at Monte Cassino, the transposition of the secular peristyle to the cloister was a natural step in the building of Europe's first monastery. His Benedictine Rule, which governed life in the monastery, set down the importance of the monastic community's self-sufficiency. Agricultural labor was a part of the daily routine. Vegetables and fruit were needed by the monastery for the table, and flowers to decorate the altar. Herbs were grown near the infirmary and reserved for healing purposes. Monte Cassino became a center for teaching medicine, which in Medieval times was practiced primarily by the clergy. During his reign as Holy Roman Emperor in the ninth century, Charlemagne compiled a list of one

Preceding:
An autumn bedding of
red salvia in the small
cloister of the Certosa of
Pavia

hundred plants to be grown in the monasteries of the empire. Our knowledge of gardening during this period is further enhanced by the existence of an extremely detailed plan for the gardens of the Swiss monastery of St. Gall.

Usually the Italian monastery had an outlying *orto* for vegetables, fruit trees, and a grape arbor. At many monasteries the abbot taught the local farmers techniques of agriculture and husbandry. Knowledge about gardening and plants was vitally preserved throughout the Dark Ages within the monastic walls. Returning crusaders and travelers often brought plants to the monasteries that offered them shelter on their journeys.

A burial ground might be combined with the orchard and could be a place for monks to walk, conversing with each other or in solitary contemplation. Often a church had a west entrance porch with a courtyard, designated a "Paradise," with flowerbeds and fruit trees. This was a spot of sanctuary for those fleeing secular persecution.

Within the walls, often attached to the church itself on the south side, was a cloister. This was a quiet haven where monks could walk in meditation, sheltered from the elements. Surrounding the open courtyard was a covered walkway, its columns standing on low walls. In central and southern Italy the columns are often encrusted with mosaic patterns, such as those found in the cloister of Monreale outside of Palermo in Sicily, and in Rome the cloister of San Paolo fuori le Mura has a riot of paired, twisted, mosaic-decorated columns. Majolica tiles were lavishly used in 1742 to decorate the cloister of Naples's Santa Chiara. Occasionally within the cloister, a garden pavilion pro-

A monk's cell garden at the Certosa of Pavia, from Triggs, The Art of Garden Design in Italy, *1906*

CERTOSA DI PAVIA   *Monks Garden.*

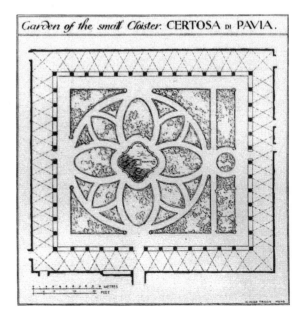

Garden of the small Cloister: CERTOSA DI PAVIA.

truded from the colonnade. Examples can be seen at Fossanova, a Cistercian convent outside of Rome, which has benches and its own fountain, and the corner pavilion set into the cloister of Monreale. Usually the center of the cloister had a well supplying the community with water for drinking, washing, and watering the plants within the walls. Later, this well or cistern was often replaced by a fountain. Occasionally there would be a *piscina,* or fishpool, for raising fish for Friday and Lenten meals. Generally the cloister garth was divided into four squares, bisected by paths edged in low box or rosemary hedges. The four paths symbolized the four streams of the river that flows through Paradise, as well as the cross itself. This division into quadrants became a constant feature of parterre design throughout the Renaissance.

Flowers were utilized for decoration of the church and for chaplets and wreaths to be worn on feast days. In Medieval days the flowers likely to be grown were the Florentine blue iris, damask and canina roses, lilies, carnations, jasmine, columbine, bellflowers, English daisies, hollyhocks, and peonies. Fruit trees might also be grown here—apples, pomegranates, sour oranges, lemons, and pears were favored. Palms and cypresses were often planted in the cloisters. The Church developed a complex symbolism associated with flowers. As many pagan deities were absorbed into Christianity, so the pagan rose of Venus and Juno's lily became symbols of the Virgin, Queen of Heaven. The red rose symbolized the blood of Christ. The pagan statues of gods and emperors within the Roman villa peristyle were replaced with those of saints and Christ.

The fourth-century church of Santi Quattro Coronati in Rome has been added to and rebuilt over the centuries. Its cloister contains

The main cloister at the Certosa of Pavia—each chimney marks a single monk's dwelling with its own garden

a real garden, lovingly tended by the Augustinian sisters who occupy the convent. The cloister was built between 1220 and 1243 by masons in memory of their fellow workers who died as Christian martyrs. At that time Santi Quattro Coronati belonged to the Benedictine Order. The cloister was restored under Pope Martin V in the fifteenth century and again in 1914 by King Victor Emmanuel III. Paired columns support the arcades surrounding the cloister garth. The columns are plain except for the colored inlay patterns lining the vaults of the arcades. Four wedge-shaped beds are set in the corners surrounding a larger central bed. A double-basined marble fountain is set in a large, well-stocked fish pool. The twelfth-century fountain with its whimsical lion masks probably originally stood in the courtyard in front of the church. The grass-filled beds are planted with roses, holly, salvia, and white and pink camellias that bloom in February.

The Franciscan cloisters have intimate, cozy gardens, often brimming over with colorful flowers. The walls are apt to be of rough stone, the scale small, the layout a simple four-part division, with a utilitarian well in the center. The small convent of San Francesco at Fiesole has two cloisters. The larger one had a wooden pergola enclosing the central well. A secondary cloister has an aviary, recalling Saint Francis's love for birds. A small pool is in the center, and a mod-

The cloister of the ancient Franciscan convent of San Damiano

est fountain is on the wall opposite the aviary. In the nineteenth century frescoes were painted under the open passageways. The church and convent of San Francesco was originally the site of an oratory, becoming a convent in 1407. Soon it was taken over by the Franciscan order which enlarged it. From 1439 it sent forth missionaries to Ethiopia and later to the Far East. Presently, it is a center for youths who are contemplating a life with the Franciscan order. The large cloister is visible through an open grill to the right of the church. It is worth the hike up the winding road from the piazza of Fiesole.

In Assisi, at San Damiano, is the tiny garden of Saint Clare, where Saint Francis composed his Canticle of the Creatures in 1225. This church was the scene of his conversion, when its large painted crucifix spoke to the saint. The cloister of San Damiano has a wide arched colonnade of warm stone. An octagonal well in the center has wrought iron with roses growing up it. Four raised flowerbeds edged in rough stone contain a profusion of flowers, including many lush pink roses. Geraniums in pots sit on the cloister walls.

Around the year 1000 Saint Romuald founded a semi-eremitical Benedictine monastery at Camaldoli in the Aretine Mountains. The site selected was on a meadow at the edge of a forest. Each monk lived in an independent hut built around a central chapel. The huts eventually were refined to contain four rooms: a chapel, studio-storeroom, bedroom, and corridor. To reach their "cell" they had to pass through a walled *orto*. In the small *orto* they would grow flowers, vegetables, and herbs for communal use. A century later, Saint Bernard, a founder of the Cistercian order in France, stressed manual agricultural labor for his monks, who were assisted by *conversi*, or lay brothers.

Monks of the Carthusian order were dedicated to silence and solitude following the rules set down by Saint Bruno in 1084. Two hundred years passed before they were permitted small gardens adjacent to their cells, which were all grouped around a central cloister. A Carthusian monastery is known as a Certosa, fine examples of which are found at Galluzzo, outside of Florence, and Pavia.

The Certosa of Galluzzo was begun in 1341. There were two grades of monks, the active laboring monks and the contemplative monks who remained in their cells in solitude, unable to speak except at Sunday communal meals. In their *ortos* the contemplative monks grew salad ingredients and other vegetables that were passed through a small opening in their cell wall and taken to the community kitchen to be cooked and distributed. The little garden could also contain a fruit tree and flowers. Each cell overlooked a tiny garden. The sixteen cells connect to a colonnaded passageway around a large grassy cloister garth. In the sixteenth century, its interior walls were frescoed by Jacopo da Pontormo. Portions of the cloister garth are fenced off as a burial ground. A sixteenth-century well stands in the center of this Renaissance cloister which was built between 1498 and 1516. The Certosa of Galluzzo was closed by the state in 1866.

Since 1958 it has been occupied by the Cistercian order. Now twelve monks inhabit the vast complex.

The Certosa of Pavia is spectacular. It has two major cloisters—one vaster than that of Galluzzo—adjacent to twenty-four cells with variously shaped chimneys. Each cell has its own garden with loggia and well in a courtyard next to the railed-off, cultivated area. The original Gothic appearance of the small cloister was updated in Renaissance style. The cloister arches have carvings by Cristoforo Mantegazza, Giovanni Antonio Amadeo, and Giovanni da Cairate. Here, too, are semibusts set in tondos as at Galluzzo. The smaller cloister is placed between the side of the church and the sixteenth-century monastery. This cloister was rebuilt between 1460 and 1470, its architect probably Giuniforte Solari. It is richly decorated with unglazed terracotta reliefs on the arches, spandrels, entablatures, and friezes. Frescoes with scenes of the Passion of Christ were painted on its inner walls. A recessed, arched lavabo of terracotta and stone is the work of Amadeo. The parterre design is slightly off center, with a basin and tiered fountain in the center of petalshaped beds. Nearby, a gate leads to herb and vegetable gardens crossed by long pergolas formed of stone columns and chestnut beams. Their destination is a fishpond.

Multistoried-arcading overlooks the cool cloister garden of Quattro Coronati

Roses growing in the simple, rough stone cloister of San Damiano at Assisi

In Piedmont, at Cioccaro di Penango, is the former convent of Sant'Uffizio. This was established in the eighteenth century for purposes of the Inquisition. The monks had a small open-air cloister, its walls formed of two rows of arching cypress creating a tunnel. Arches were cut curving inward onto the small cloister garth, and small exterior windows looked out on the rolling countryside of the Montferrat region. The green surrounding tunnel has been opened up and unfortunately clipped. The central fountain, formerly operated by a hand pump, is now a simple basin. The parterre, however, has kept its original Baroque form and is filled with flowers. An adjacent kitchen garden is planted with flowers for cutting and filled with purple iris in the spring. The convent of Sant'Uffizio was closed in 1860. For the past twenty-odd years the property has been run as a fine restaurant, now expanded as a charming inn in the capable hands of the Firato family. The gardens are meticulously kept up by an elderly gardener who clings to old methods. The only jarring note is the use of obtrusive lighting fixtures in the gardens.

Renaissance Palace Gardens

Renaissance Palaces are all open to the public:

Palazzo del Tè, Mantua

Palazzo Piccolomini, Pienza (gardens visible from palace windows)

Palazzo Ducale, Urbino (gardens visible from palace windows)

Palazzo Ducale, Mantua

Castello Estense, Ferrara

Palazzo Medici-Riccardi, Florence

The glow of late afternoon sun bathes the hanging garden of Palazzo Piccolomini

A number of urban Renaissance courtyard gardens have come down to us intact. These are intimate gardens, confined within palace walls, sheltered from the noise and confusion of the outside world. They are adapted from the cloister garden and geometrical in layout, although the religious images here are sometimes replaced with pagan ones. Often the surrounding peristyle has been shifted to an upper floor, which looks down on the garden. The sounds of central fountains, birds, and rustling of foliage remain, but the recitation of prayers has been replaced by secular conversation and music. Some,

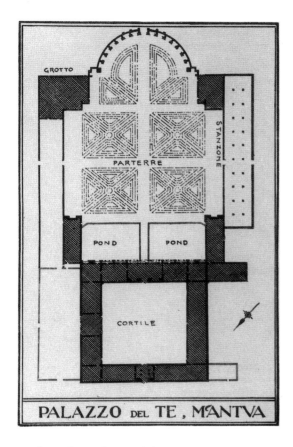

PALAZZO DEL TE, MANTVA

such as the Palazzo del Tè at Mantua and Palazzo Medici in Florence, are inward-looking; others have balconies overlooking the city, as at Ferrara. The Palazzo Piccolomini at Pienza and the Ducal Palace of Urbino look over the surrounding countryside, providing an example for the siting of Renaissance villas on hilltops to take advantage of pleasant breezes and panoramic views. Transitional in nature, these small gardens are part of the development of the Classic Italian garden.

The Castello Estense in Ferrara is a Medieval fortress which became the principal residence of the ruling Este family under Duke Ercole I in the late fifteenth and early sixteenth centuries. The duke added a story to the fortress, connecting it to the ducal palace. His successor, Alfonso I, constructed the roof garden early in the sixteenth century. A graceful small loggia opens on the courtyard. Originally this garden was filled with orange trees in pots. Now on the marble pedestals stand palm trees. The Este family was famous for its intellectual court; poets, philosophers, and musicians gathered here. Ferrara under the Este had spectacular gardens in and around the city, including that of Belfiore, il Barchetto, and Montagnola—

each linked together by allées. Regrettably, all have vanished with time.

The hanging garden of the Ducal Palace at Urbino is enclosed by high walls of the palace on three sides. The vast, rectangular terrace is badly neglected at present, but merits restoration. Created by the architect Luciano Laurana for Duke Federico da Montefeltro between 1468 and 1472, it was first described by Bernardino Baldi in 1480. The garden was divided into square raised flowerbeds with stone bases in their centers for flower-filled urns. Trelliswork with ivy and jasmine softened the walls, against which were stone benches.

The frescoed loggia of the secret garden at Palazzo del Tè

In the heart of Florence the garden of Palazzo Medici-Riccardi is kept up today. This is on the ground floor, opening off the entrance courtyard. The garden must date from the second quarter of the fifteenth century, but has been altered. Up until 1494, when the Medici were expelled from the city, the garden contained important sculpture, including the bronze statue of Judith and Holofernes by Donatello, designed as a fountain for this garden (it is believed that wine flowed from it for festive occasions). Michelangelo sculpted a snow giant here after a freak snowstorm. The palace borders the garden on two walls; an upper loggia looks down on it at one end. The opposite end is closed by a *limonaia*, or lemon greenhouse. Pebble designs appear in the paths, and the grassy flowerbeds are set with potted lemon trees.

The hanging garden of Palazzo Piccolomini in Pienza was much admired in its time. The palace and its garden were designed in 1460 by Bernardo Rossellino for the Piccolomini pope, Pius II. The vista of the Val d'Orcia was intended to be visible upon entering the palazzo; the entrance, courtyard gate to the garden, and center arch of the garden wall are placed on an axis. The garden is gracefully incorporated into the palazzo, which encloses it on three sides. The fourth side is an ivy-covered wall pierced by three arches, providing views of the rolling countryside. Here at last, the garden begins to move out of confining interior walls, opening beyond the palace itself. This concept was influential in the planning of subsequent villas. The stone is honey-colored, warming the sheltered garden, which consists of four raised beds. Along the sides are raised beds planted with irises. At the crossing is a small marble fountain; a well is tucked in the northwest corner.

The Palazzo del Tè was built for a summer pleasure residence for the Gonzaga Duke Federico II. Charles Dickens described it in 1844 as "that exhausted cistern of a Palace, among the reeds and rushes, with the mists hovering about outside, and stalking round and round it continually" (*Pictures From Italy,* 1844). The palace, after long neglect, has been carefully restored. The garden is still damp and, as yet, has not been spruced up to its former grandeur. The vast courtyard, once planted with intricate parterres, is now reduced to large stretches of lawn divided by gravel paths. Its interest lies in

Palazzo del Tè: the fish-pond bordering the casino

the layout: steps lead from the courtyard of the palace up to a loggia; from there the garden extends, reached by traversing a bridge over fish pools. At the far end is a large hemicycle of open arches, extending the garden vista into the surrounding marshes. This large garden was first planned as an open room rather than a parterre area. Here were held displays of horsemanship, balls, concerts, poetry recitations, and in the fish pools, *naumachia*, or mock sea battles. Later, the parterres were flanked with pleached allées and ornamented with statuary—all vanished now. To the right, flanking the former parterre, is a *limonaia*. To the left of the hemicycle is a secret garden with a delicate frescoed loggia at one end. A center path leads to a rustic grotto at the far end. Red poppies grow haphazardly before the portal of *spugne*, artificial texturing in imitation of cave walls. Rolling the wooden doors aside, one enters a two-chambered grotto, in process of being restored. Its walls are covered with shells, colored stones, and painted stucco. The mosaics depict white ducks, a flaming urn, and a stork in a burning nest. A large rustic fountain once gurgled on hot summer days. Mantua, like Ferrara, is a town of once important Renaissance gardens that have since vanished. Both cities suffered from invading armies; Palazzo del Tè was heavily damaged during the wars of succession in 1629 and again from 1702 through 1708 when Imperial troops sacked the city. All these ducal palaces are open to the public, their gardens visible.

I *Piedmont*
Lombardy
Veneto

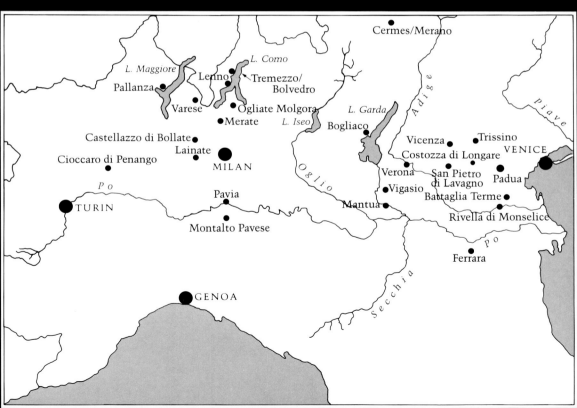

Cermes/Merano

L. Maggiore

L. Como

Lenno

Pallanza

Tremezzo/
Bolvedro

Varese

Ogliate Molgora

L. Garda

Merate

L. Iseo

Bogliaco

Adige

Piave

Castellazzo di Bollate

Vicenza

Trissino

Lainate

Costozza di Longare

VENICE

Cioccaro di Penango

MILAN

Verona

San Pietro
di Lavagno

Padua

Oglio

Po

Vigasio

Pavia

Battaglia Terme

TURIN

Mantua

Rivella di Monselice

Montalto Pavese

Po

Ferrara

Secchia

GENOA

Villa Toeplitz

Varese
Gardens open to the public

On a residential hillside of Varese is a Classic Italian garden with a modern flavor. After visiting nearby Baroque gardens, the Villa Toeplitz leaves a somewhat surreal impression. The traditional rules are observed for an axial formal garden that dissolves into woods, with parterres, a water cascade, and symmetrical garden rooms. Yet the materials are modern, and vast lawns—seldom seen in Italy—flow up into the formal garden, merging it with a landscape park of magnificent specimen trees.

The cascade is starkly modern—no softening edges or patinas of moss. It is bordered on either side by steps, the risers filled with gravel. Water flows from a cypress-crowned hillside, beneath a belvedere, down a steep slope, to a flat parterre area. Two large rectangular beds have *broderie* ("embroidered" or arabesque-shaped) patterns of low box set in warm-colored pebbles. On either side garden rooms are enclosed by arches of trained yew. Massed conifers stand behind them as a backdrop. Beyond the parterre is a fountain surrounded by round mounds of ivy and planted with tulips in the spring. The cascade continues down the sloping lawn; metal paddles that move with the water catch the light and add a new dimension to the sights and sounds of the garden.

The entryway from Viale dei Toeplitz is not the original site of the entrance. The long iron fence that originally surrounded the park was destroyed in World War II. An allée of limes brings the visitor to the water garden on the left and an arboretum on the right. A small gravel terrace garden extends behind the villa. Further on is a green garden of lawns and clipped hedges with a rectangular reflecting pool.

The gardens near the villa date from between 1918 and 1928. A German built the villa around 1900, living here under surveillance during World War I. In 1925 Giuseppe Toeplitz, a Polish-born banker, purchased the property. He had the water garden built before his death in 1935. Large plants were shipped from nurseries in Pistoia, and he installed night illumination. From 1945 until 1972 the garden was owned by a textile industrialist who restored the cascade and walls and rewired the garden lighting. Since then, the garden has belonged to the city of Varese and is open as a public park.

A view of the formal garden from the slopes of the water cascade

Right:
Water flows through the channel via propelling paddles—a modern version of the Baroque cascade

35 · *Villa Toeplitz*

Castello Balduino

Montalto Pavese
Gardens may be open upon
request:
Conte Balduino
Via Santa Margherita a
Montici 44
Florence

A fresco of Castello Balduino, showing the original design of the gardens

Castello Balduino is a world unto itself. After the open terrain of the Lombardy terrain, hills begin to gradually rise along country roads, twenty miles south of Pavia and six miles east of Voghera. The road winds through vineyards progressively swelling with the beautiful colors of autumn. The castle gates are just before the village of Montalto Pavese. Beyond a whimsical gatehouse, the road bends upward, past loosely clipped hedges tended by an elderly gardener. One climbs up through a park planted with a variety of trees, including old poplars, cypresses, and assorted conifers. Pheasants strut beneath

Virginia creeper growing over a statue

The belvedere overlooking the geometric topiary gardens

branches and truffles lie hidden beneath the moist ground. At the summit the castle stands fifteen hundred feet above sea level.

A long, unbroken façade of mellowed brick with faded blue shutters is bordered by undulating beds of closely clipped yew. In their centers stand weathered statues of warriors on pedestals. From the broad terrace is a spectacular view of the hills of the Oltre Po region. To the right is a small belvedere, to the left, staircases lead down into the garden proper. This terrace affords the best view of the topiary parterres below.

There are two gardens densely filled with carved yew; the shapes resemble chess set pieces. The right garden is designed within a square. A pattern of cubical shapes with low domes radiates outward in a star. Within low border parterres are rounded mounds of yew. The adjacent garden is longer, double the length, with a central path in the center and similar domed cubes in yew. Here the layout is more spacious, with intricate, low, broad parterre designs at the four corners. The garden terminates beyond high hornbeam hedges. Its central path continues through two large cypresses to a semicircular belvedere terrace, which once overlooked a tennis court, now transformed into a plant nursery. To the right of this terrace is a *boschetto* (a little wood) with small stone tree stumps under the real

Diana, goddess of the hunt

trees. Returning to the castle, one passes through a hornbeam tunnel bordering the eastern side of the long topiary garden.

The castle courtyard is enclosed on three sides, the western side remaining open with a balustraded belvedere. This overlooks a semi-circular parterre with a central fountain of Pan. A sheltered walk hugs the bulwark of the courtyard. Against the walls are box hedges with geraniums; two rows of lemon trees are set on supporting walls, the box hedges recessed for pot placement. Beneath the belvedere is a greenhouse with a statue of Diana. Occasionally, the hills of the Oltre Po are covered with snow, and then, of course, the lemon trees are brought in for the winters.

The original part of the castle was a Medieval look-out tower. Cardinal Belcredi made it into a fortress to defend the town; subse-quently, in 1735, it was transformed into a villa. Giovanni Antonio Veneroni, an architect of Pavia, drew up plans for Marchese Antonio Belcredi, which show the projected garden dating from this time. Defense walls were torn down and, where possible, the ground leveled to create gardens. Portions of the garden apparently were never real-ized, but what survives today closely follows Veneroni's designs.

In 1850 the castle was sold to the Benvenuti family, who did not maintain it properly. When the Balduino family bought it in 1909 it was in need of serious restoration. The following year they called in the architect Giovanni Chevaliere who added small wings to form the courtyard. The gardens were lovingly restored according to the eighteenth-century designs. Today the property is owned by Count Cesare Balduino. The parterres are still carefully clipped, but they lack flowers, and statues are toppling. With minimal work these mar-velous topiary gardens could be brought back to their former glory.

Villa San Remigio

*Pallanza, Lake Maggiore
Gardens open to the public
mornings*

*A Roman-style wall foun-
tain set with mosaics*

*Right:
The Giardino dei Sospiri
with Venus driving her
sea chariot*

Between the towns of Intra and Pallanza on Lake Maggiore is a residential zone, Castagnola. A road winding up the hill of this neighbor-
hood leads to the entrance of the villa and its park. Here is a series
of terraced gardens conceived in 1883 by a romantic couple steeped in
the atmosphere of Gabriele D'Annunzio. Each garden was intended
to evoke a specific emotion. Architecturally, the couple imitated the
style of seventeenth-century Italy when they built their villa and
planned the gardens.

In 1859 an Englishman, Peter Browne, settled here with his family, building a chalet on the hillside overlooking the lake. His neigh-
bor, the marquis Federico della Valle di Casanova, owned the adjacent
fields and eventually married Browne's daughter. Federico's son, Silvio, in turn married Browne's granddaughter Sophie. The garden is
the creation of Silvio and Sophie. Work on the terraces towards the
lake began in 1883. Sophie made a model of the garden which she
placed in the moonlight to test out the effects. They replaced the

Creamy roses grow over the balcony of the Giardino della Memoria

chalet with the loggiaed villa, and then finally in 1905 created a terrace behind the villa, high up on the hillside overlooking Lake Maggiore. The garden was completed in 1916. An army of thirty gardeners kept it in pristine condition until Sophie died in 1960, at age one hundred. It is now owned by the Regione Piedmonte and operated as a school. As in Sophie's day, the garden is accessible to the public, although it is beginning to deteriorate, the stonework crumbling.

The entrance drive winds through a park, planted with azaleas and rhododendrons under ash, chestnuts, and ancient oaks. The bottom terrace is the Giardino della Mestizia—the Melancholy Garden. The niche in the center of its far wall contains a statue of Hercules and the Hydra signed by Giovani Marchiori; this marks the bottom axis of the garden. Ironwork surrounds rectangular patches of lawn. Classical statues, worn stone lions, urns once filled with myrtle, and a square basin decorate this level. Marchioness Sophie's painting studio was built here against the retaining wall, alongside a *nymphaeum*—a grotto dedicated to nymphs. The worn statues, planted solely with green plant material, and the stately calm of the garden perhaps evoked sadness to the della Valle family.

The next level up was the Giardino dei Sospiri—Garden of Sighs. This is dominated by a large curving basin, with a life-size sculpture by Riccardo Ripamonti of Venus on a large seashell driving her sea-

Giardino dei Sospiri

horses. Against the wall are niches with statues of a cavalier with his sword and a lady in a farthingale, a shepherdess and Silenus, the wise tutor to Dionysus. Parterres with low box borders are planted with roses between paths set with fleur-de-lis pebble patterns. Stone benches invite contemplation. Wrought-iron balconies overlook the lowest level of the garden. Two flights of steps lead to the next level.

The Giardino della Memoria—Memory Garden—has a balustrade topped with statues and pyramids. A flintstone arch is covered with roses. Statues of three putti dance in a rectangular flowerbed, and tall columns surmounted by pinecones stand on this terrace. A wrought-iron gate leads to woods off to the side. At one time, Sophie grew white roses, trained in garlands, and red flowers spilled out of urns. The *limonaia* (lemon greenhouse) is built against the hillside. On either side of it steps lead up to the next terrace.

The Giardino delle Ore—Garden of the Hours—has a central sundial and a statue gesturing for silence. On the balustrade are statues of Pluto, Venus, Bacchus, and Juno attributed to Orazio Marinali. An inscription informs us that the sundial was placed there by Silvio and Sophie to mark the sunny hours brought on by the dawn, which drove away the shadows of night. On the same level is a *limonaia* with a grotto containing a stream. Eighteenth-century statues by Francesco Rizzi stand on the wall above it.

Central steps lead to a small *hortus conclusus,* a "Roman"-walled narrow garden room situated directly below the double staircase to the villa itself. Etruscan tombs stand against the ivy-covered walls. Four columned, mosaic-encrusted niches are built into the retaining wall with patterns of dolphins and garlands. A yew is trimmed in the shape of an armchair contrasting with four stone chairs formed by dolphins supporting seashells. Sophie's beloved roses continue to grow in this sheltered spot.

Villa la Quiete

Between Tremezzo and
Bolvedro, Lake Como
Gardens closed to the public,
but visible from road

Villa la Quiete, also known as Villa Sola, has a perfectly intact parterre design from the early eighteenth century. The terrace seems like
a carpet set before the lakeside when seen from an upper window of
the villa. This is a parterre of four broad segments with *broderie*
(elaborate arabesque) patterns composed entirely of green lawn set off
by pebble designs. The smooth, colored pebbles are permanently
placed in cement. Flowerbeds of white begonias, ageratum, or yellow
pansies edge the walls of the villa. The white gravel paths contrast
with the grass and blue water of the Gulf of San Lorenzo. An ivy-
covered wall runs along the side of the garden, but the end of the garden is bordered by a low balustrade and decorative wrought-iron gate
topped with statues and stone urns. The absence of a high wall unites
the lake to the garden and creates an unforgettable scene. The parterre is entirely visible from the road running between the garden and
the graceful steps of the boat landing. The property is not extensive.
A small shady park exists to the left of the villa, but its larger trees
were destroyed in a recent hurricane.

The villa was built around 1700 by the Duchess Del Carretto. It
then became the property of the Brentano family, who passed it on
to Duke Gian Galeazzo Serbelloni. Gian Galeazzo had a larger villa
at Bellagio across the lake; this he reserved as a guest house. The present appearance of the villa dates from his ownership. One of its oc-
cupants was the Abbot Giuseppe Parini, who was hired as tutor to
the Serbelloni sons. The famous poet probably composed "Mattino"
here, which instructed young men on how to employ their morning
hours. Gian Galeazzo gave the villa to his only daughter, Luisa, as
part of her dowry when she married Marquis Lodovico Busca. In 1871
the villa again passed in marriage when Antonella Busca married
Count Andrea Sola. Her son Gian Ludovico had three daughters, one
of whom, Countess Sola Cabiati, was mayoress of the nearby town
Tremezzo. At her death, the villa was left to her two sisters.

Villa la Quiete was once well-named for its solitude and calm
vista of the lake; now, unfortunately, much traffic passes before its
gates.

Following:
Pink roses swathe a gar-
den lamp post above
colored pebble patterns

Villa Balbianello

*Lenno, Lake Como
Gardens open to the public
April to October on Tuesdays,
Saturdays, Sundays
Access by boat only, from
Ossuccio*

*Ornate stone balustrade
of Balbianello*

Balbianello covers the end of the promontory Dosso di Lavedo, jutting out into the center of Lake Como—the site is dreamlike. From the summit it is possible to see all three parts of the lake—the northern shore, Como, and Lecco. Cars are not permitted to approach the villa by the one-way private drive that circumvents the mountain. The visitor must arrive by boat to a rose-covered landing on the southern side. In addition, the tip of the promontory has a delicious little port, protected by a wall with statues of religious figures, including Saint Carlo Borromeo blessing the lapping waters.

The land drops sharply away on three sides; on the fourth, the terrain rises unevenly. This irregularity dictated terracing and ruled out formal parterres. The plant material is a mixture of seaside and mountain vegetation, made possible by the mild climate. Cypresses, plane trees, laurel, azaleas, wild pines, and palms all flourish.

Founded as a place of worship in the thirteenth century under the Franciscans, the villa evolved into a summer residence for prel-

*Clipped trees line the
path leading to the land-
ing stage*

ates. On the promontory Paolo Giovio built the Villa di Campo in 1540. It remained in the hands of the Church, counting among its guests Giovanni Angelo de' Medici (Pope Pius IV from 1559 to 1565). In 1787 the papal legate Cardinal Angelo Maria Durini became its owner. Cardinal Durini purchased the adjacent property at the end of the promontory comprising the oratory and convent. In 1790 he built a new villa, and at the crest of the hill he erected a graceful loggia. In the nineteenth century the property passed to the families of Porro Lambertenghi and Arconati Visconti. The Arconati held it for about a century. Balbianello became a hub of anti-Austrian activity. Writer-patriot Silvio Pellico was seized here prior to his nine-year imprisonment in Austria's fortress of Spielburg. The property was then purchased by the American general Butler Ames in 1919. Balbianello was a wonderful stage set for the general's wife, Fifi Ames, known locally as the Signora della Fucsia. She could be seen descending the steps of the miniature port, all dressed in sweeping white, wearing fresh fuchsia blossoms as earrings and a corsage. At that time the garden was a riot of flowers in all colors. After the general's death, his heirs sold Balbianello to Count Guido Monzino in 1974. Monzino made major repairs, lovingly restoring every detail. Count Monzino was an intrepid explorer. He made an expedition to the North Pole in 1971 and climbed Mount Everest two years later. His tomb is in the garden that he loved. At his death, the property passed to the Fondo Ambiente Italiano, which maintains it impeccably today, while making it accessible to the public.

The visitor is greeted at the landing by pink azaleas, santolina, box, and yellow and white roses growing on the iron gate. Red impatiens grows on the rocky wall. Ancient plane trees shade the gravel walk leading to the terrace, which serves as a mock bastion, with four small canons pointing out towards the lake. A small courtyard filled with jasmine leads to the entrance of the villa. In the courtyard is a marble fireplace mantel with caryatid figures and a statue of a warrior. Passing through the hallway, one exits out into the garden. A broad lawn is bounded by one of the carved stone balustrades—the trademark of Balbianello. Seesawing putti are interspersed with the Visconti emblem—a snake devouring a child. On this northern side, the cliff drops to the water's edge. Hydrangeas bloom on this terrace. Beyond, reached by a flight of steps, is Monzino's tomb, a bronze slab inscribed with his many achievements. Steps continue steeply upward to reach the loggia. Here coffee was served for the first time in Italy. Trained laurel grows against the loggia. The hillside rises up to a caretaker's cottage. Beneath it statues are set in a sea of pink azaleas amid sloping, finely manicured lawns. A path curves and sweeps down to the boat landing. The name Balbianello was given by Cardinal Durini to this point, in deference to the Balbianos, a prominent family in the area.

A statue of Flora stands against the hills of Lake Como

Following:
The lush colors of azaleas are intensified by May showers

Villa Bettoni

Bogliaco, Lake Garda
Gardens closed to the public,
but visible from road

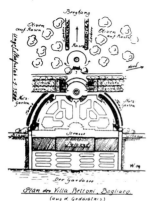

The garden of Villa Bettoni is visible from the western shore road of Lake Garda. The stately lakeside villa was built on land owned by the counts Bettoni since the fifteenth century. The garden and villa were commissioned by Count Giovanni Antonio Bettoni, cavalry commander of the empress of Austria, Maria Theresa. The villa sits on a terrace by the water's edge; its central block is four stories high and topped by a balustrade decorated with mythological statues by Giovanni Battista Locatelli. The side wings each have a bridge spanning the main road, connecting the villa to the garden. The southern wing already existed in the seventeenth century. The central portion was begun in 1751, designed by the Veronese architect Adriano Cristofari. A northern wing was added to balance its counterpart. Five years later, after disagreements with the architect, the work was handed over to Antonio Marchetti of Brescia. Work continued until the end of the century.

Seen from the road, the garden is constructed like a stage set, rising up against the hillside. A broad lawn, divided into six large green parterre segments and gravel walks, is bordered on the right and left by evergreen hedges. These hedges are set above low walls ornamented with stone vases. At the rear a massive *nymphaeum* (a grotto once dedicated to nymphs) is criss-crossed by ramps. The ground level ramps curve, forming a small piazza with a grotto. Three arched openings face a circular fish basin. Niches with stone statuary by Locatelli decorate the *nymphaeum*'s surface. A balustrade broken in the center crowns the structure.

In the winter the topmost level is enclosed, transformed into a green house to protect the lemon trees. This shore of the lake has long been famous for its lemon production. At the top a short flight of steps leads to a semicircular wall, whose niches are graced by vases. Behind is an allée of cypresses, set within the olive grove. It was intended to lead to a temple dedicated to Apollo, which was never realized.

Opposite the main body of the villa is the entrance gate to the garden. This section of the garden has only recently been restored—magnificently. Judging by a sketched plan of the garden from 1910, the parterre shapes have been altered. The lakeside garden consists of grassy rosebeds with a central flowerbed in front of the vine-covered entrance portal. Two low, balustraded wings frame the garden, which opens onto the lake.

*The stuccoed garden theater-*limonaia *freshly restored in cream with peach accents*

Villa Sommi-Picenardi

Ogliate Molgora
Gardens may be open upon
request:
Marchesa Alessandra Sommi-
Picenardi
Via Marco Sommi-Picenardi 8
Ogliate Molgora (Como)

There is a pastoral quality about the Villa Sommi-Picenardi, surrounded by its peaceful nineteenth-century landscape park. Around the side and back are two formal gardens from the previous century, still beautifully preserved. Each is like a stage set, well-viewed from within the villa, whose windows frame the gardens like a proscenium. On occasion, the rear garden is duplicated in miniature as a centerpiece for special dinner parties.

The property once belonged to the Vimercate family, then the Sala Trotti acquired it in 1678. It now belongs to Marchioness Alessandra Sommi-Picenardi.

The villa dates from the eighteenth century, incorporating an earlier tower. The southern block was torn down, opening the courtyard in the nineteenth century. In front of the villa is a spectacular plane tree, at least 150 years old, whose roots extend under the front hall of the villa.

Rounding the corner of the villa one comes upon the green theater, all in box, with tall side hedges of hornbeam cut with arched openings for entrances and exits of the actors. The stage consists of narrow, gently terraced levels. The theater is planted on a slight rise, narrowing at the top to appear longer than it is.

From the theater a green tunnel leads to the rear terraced garden. This formal garden was laid out by the Sala Trotti family in the latter part of the eighteenth century. Bordering the villa is a rectangular lawn with central fountains of small bronze seahorses. The rising hillside is laid out in eight terraces with holly hedges; the sustaining walls are covered in ivy. In the center, on an axis with the villa, is an exquisite staircase rising from a parterre. This staircase is decorated with panels of colored pebbles and beautiful balustrades in the styles of Louis XIV and XVI with festoons of laurel. The walls and balustrades are topped with stone vases filled with coleus. Steep steps lead up the hill, past pampas grass and statues to a backdrop at the summit of cypress trees. Further on are two high cypresses with a little table and chair overlooking a pasture, now used for horses which roam freely over the forty acres of park.

During the late nineteenth century the gardens were restored and the English landscape garden created. The rear garden probably acquired its lawn and central pool at this time, as well. The owner, then, was a lady in waiting to Queen Margherita, whose court resided at Monza. When the villa's dining room was restored in 1886 the queen was invited to dinner, the first of several pleasant visits.

The monumental staircase in the rear garden is accented by pampas grass and a row of cypresses

Villa Belgioioso

Merate
Gardens open upon request:
Marchese Brivio Sforza,
Via Olmetto 17
Milan

The garden at Villa Belgioioso in its present form is an intriguing exercise in the use of evergreen plant material to create a vast outdoor salon. With sweeping staircases, beautifully carved balustrades, and surrounding hornbeam tunnels, the enclosed lawn becomes an extension of the villa itself—a typically Italian garden design element.

It is rare to find a famed garden that has been redesigned and replanted with such successful results. Only a tiny portion of the original garden remains today—the parterre of the aviary, adjacent to the villa, which in the past was the commencement of the formal descending gardens. The rest has been swept away, transformed into an English landscape park, or restructured as a large garden room.

Arriving from the village of Merate, the narrow ascending road widens into a minipiazza with large, wrought-iron gates on either side. This *piazzetta* is called the Atrio Belgioioso, dating from the 1770s.

To the left the gate leads down an overgrown allée, the former approach to the stately villa. When the new road was made, the end

Engraving by Dal Re, Ville di delizia, *1726. Only the uppermost portion of the garden survives today*

An example of one of the Baroque statues in the rich collection at Villa Belgioioso

of the cypress allée was transformed into a perspective hemicycle. Here a Neoclassical rotonda was designed by Leopoldo Pollak in 1791.

The opposite gate sets off the entrance courtyard to the present villa, built in the early eighteenth century on the site of a thirteenth-century convent. Existing water rights date back to the foundation of the convent. These are important for the maintenance of the garden today. In 1540 the Novati acquired the property; it was then revamped two centuries later by the Milanese architect Giacomo Muttone for Marquis Ferrante Villani-Novati. The original garden to the plan of Muttone is depicted in Marcantonio Dal Re's *Ville di delizia*, dated 1726. This consisted of a series of seven descending terraces linked by staircases, including one in a handsome horseshoe design at the fifth level. The garden was walled, ending in an evergreen *exedra*, or open-air niche. The lowest terrace was subdivided into three sections: the center had a large oval fishpond with high water jet; to the left was an intricate maze, balanced on the right by a small green theater. Early in the nineteenth century, the wings of the enormous villa were eliminated and important alterations took place in the gardens. With the exception of the uppermost garden terrace, all the descending levels were destroyed.

When Marquis Ferrante Villani-Novati died in 1749, the villa was acquired by Countess Barbara d'Adda. It was subsequently owned by Prince Antonio Barbiano di Belgioioso and eventually passed to a cousin, Prince Trivulzio. In the twentieth century Princess Marianna Trivulzio married Marquis Annibale Brivio Sforza. Don Luigi Brivio Sforza inherited the villa in 1989.

The Belgioiosos created the French-style garden between 1773 and 1774, according to Don Alessandro Brivio Sforza, to provide employment for the local population in a time of famine. It was designed on a direct axis with the villa, and borrowed the idea of unfolding perspective viewpoints from André le Nôtre. The architect is unknown.

The arched tunnels of hornbeam have been likened to Bernini's colonnade in front of Saint Peter's in Rome. Below the villa's terrace, the parallel walls of greenery swell into a hemicycle embracing a grassy lawn. This terminates in a belvedere framing the vista of the park below. The plan called for a large reflecting pool in the hemicycle, but the proposed weight of the water threatened the substructure of the knoll, so a subtle declivity in the lawn is all that remains of this idea.

Light filters through the hornbeam tunnels, revealing small side chambers, like the former garden rooms at Versailles. These tunnels are clipped once a year by three men, who work meticulously, sighting the "string course"—one on a ladder, another on the ground, and the third at a distance to ensure an even line. The clipping takes sixteen full days. At the turn of the century colored pebbles and black coal picked out the coat of arms of the Belgioioso family on the lawn near the terrace. Each spring, twenty workers would come to put the garden in order, cutting the grass with scythes.

The garden suffered greatly in the last war. In recent years the sandstone statues and balustrades have been restored and treated with protective compresses. These sculptures and railings were salvaged from the original eighteenth-century garden and are of high quality.

To the right of the terrace is a small rectangular formal garden

The surviving section of the original garden showing the voliera *and rustic "wooden" fence in stone*

with raised flowerbeds and a small fountain in a quatrefoil basin. This
is the only intact remnant of the original eighteenth-century garden.
At the far end is a *voliera*, or aviary, with frescoed scenes of a deer
chase within its arches. Mosaic decorates the exterior. Vases are filled
with fuchsia and orange trees. Bordering this garden are stone balustrades in imitation of tree trunks, a charming conceit. The garden's
steps, which formerly led to a series of successive formal terraces,
now end at a lily pond and a small niche containing a fountain of a
faun. Extending before it is the English park, created in 1837 by Giuseppe Balzaretti.

Villa Visconti Borromeo Litta Toselli

Lainate
Gardens open to the public

*Mythological group in
terracotta*

The French-style gardens of nearby Villa Arconati Crivelli inspired
the eighteenth-century Villa Visconti Borromeo Litta Toselli. Similar
in scale, the Villa Litta is important for its surviving pavilions, which
provide clues to those destroyed at Castellazzo.

The villa was completed by 1569 for Fabio Visconti Borromeo
and subsequently inherited by Pirro Visconti Borromeo. The original
design of the garden dates from this time and was extended and ornamented by Pirro's successors. In 1750, after the death of Giulio Visconti Borromeo Arese, the property went to his nephew, Pompeo
Litta. Under the Littas the garden flourished and was expanded until
the beginning of the nineteenth century.

The garden has three sections. The first is in line with the villa
to the southwest. It consists of a field, bordered with hornbeam,
which ends in a hemicycle. Parallel to this is a large rectangular section, its cross-divided parterre now effaced, with a fountain of Tritons
in the center. Two large greenhouses border it to the north. Beyond
this is a swath of English landscape garden laid out by Pietro Cano-
nica in the nineteenth century with free-form paths. The third and
most interesting section is in the northeast area of the garden. It consists of a large formal parterre garden in two sections with fanciful
pavilions framing the main area. The adjacent smaller portion had
the more complex parterre pattern and opened onto the public road.
It, too, was bordered by buildings at the ends to tie the composition
together. A long white pavilion at the south end of the large parterre
is a work of pure fantasy; pebble-encrusted grottoes are adorned with
spugne (imitation stalactites), frescoes, mosaics, statuary, and belvederes set on raised terraces with pebbled, diamond-patterned pave-
ments. The grotto complex has a central room decorated with water
tricks, frescoes, and *spugne.* It faces onto the parterre with a central
fountain of Galatea, sculpted in 1785 by Donato Carabelli—an elaborate Neoclassical concoction. Nymphs recline, one mysteriously
veiled, upon an outer balustrade above the fountain. Opposite the
grotto is a pavilion once used as a greenhouse. In its center is a niche
of *spugne* with a terracotta statue of three struggling figures.

The garden as a whole has a disjointed effect; the parterre of the

grotto pavilion is on a seventy-eight-degree angle to the portion aligned with the villa. Perhaps the parts destroyed to create the English garden had helped to correct this imbalance.

The Littas enhanced the villa for a century, attracting to their home famous personages of the day. The poet Giuseppe Parini dedicated "Il dono, la recita dei versi," and "Inclita Nice" to the Litta sisters, Paola Castiglioni and Maria Castelbarco. The Litta brothers, Antonio and Giulio, favored a unified Italy and, after an uprising in Milan, were exiled by the reigning Austrians. They returned to Lainate in 1859 on the day following the Battle of Magenta, in which Italian and French forces defeated the Austrians. Unfortunately, Antonio contracted large debts, and at his death in 1860 the property was seized by the public treasury.

In 1872 Baron Ignazio Weil-Weiss bought the villa and carefully restored it. The Toselli family acquired the villa in 1932 and once again restored it, but after World War II it was abandoned. In the early 1970s the villa was bought by the town of Lainate with the intent to restore the property. The villa is now a combination of police headquarters and town offices. The present approach is through a squalid parking lot and side wall. The garden is partially overgrown and untended. The large greenhouses stand empty before the wide field, whose paths have vanished, but the large white marble fountain of Neptune and his Tritons is still there. However, the rear formal garden of Galatea has been wonderfully restored by the Soprintendenza dei Monumenti. The fountain plays again, and the parterres are maintained. Work continues on the complex of grottoes, but the opposite pavilions are open and used as a small informal museum of the villa's history and a gathering spot for local residents. The renaissance of these gardens is very satisfying; the grotto pavilion is important in the history of Italian gardens, and it is a pleasure to see the garden lived in once again.

*A small parterre within
the large formal garden*

*Right:
The Fountain of Galatea
by Donato Carabelli*

Villa Arconati Crivelli

Castellazzo di Bollate
Gardens closed to the public

There is an air of fading splendor about the Villa Arconati Crivelli. It sits proudly, like an island of the past, surrounded by the squalid suburbs of Milan. The owner, Marchioness Beatrice Crivelli Sormani-Verri, is in her eighties and has long loved this property, keeping it up over the years. Unfortunately, her son's interests lie elsewhere and the villa was put up for sale. I visited a month before it was due to be sold to a consortium. It had just had most of its evergreens clipped for the final time, and the following week straw and burlap were to be laid over the pebble mosaics to protect them from the winter freeze. The state does not allow the garden to be destroyed or built over, but it could vanish through neglect and vandalism. This would be a tragedy, because this is one of the great French-inspired Lombard gardens of the eighteenth century. It is a rare survivor, albeit imperfectly preserved.

Time has eliminated the great parterre which now appears as a long, flat lawn, punctuated by topiary candelabra. The present impression is of a green garden: almost all flowers have been deleted. This is understandable considering the vast extent of the garden tended by only two gardeners.

The villa passed through several families, beginning with the Cusani and then the extremely rich counts of Arconati. After three generations of Arconati brought the villa to its present size, the direct male line died out and the property passed by the female line to the Busca, then to the Sormani, and finally to the Crivelli family.

The villa itself evolved from an older Medieval block, which is now a museum; additions in the shape of a large H brought it to its full form. Incorporated in the older section of the villa is the church of San Guglielmo, restored in 1573 by the Cusani on the occasion of a visit by San Carlo Borromeo, archbishop of Milan. In the first half of the seventeenth century the villa was expanded with a U-shaped addition, probably on a design of Martino Bassi. Part of the garden that exists today dates from this time. Records in the Arconati family archives describe how oxen pulled loads of statuary and fountains from Rome in 1627 for the garden planned for Count Galeazzo Arconati. The gardens were conceived of as extensions of the villa, de-

Plan from Triggs, The Art of Garden Design in Italy, *1906*

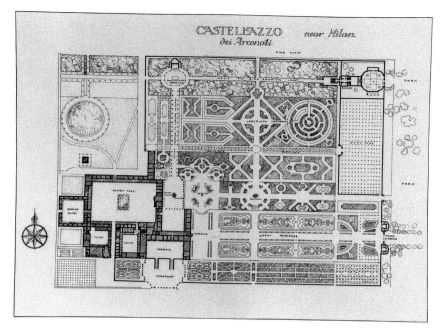

signed as a series of small-scale garden rooms placed on an axis with the villa's carriage entrance to the east and the colonnaded courtyard to the north. The main entrance cut through cultivated fields to the south—as it still does today.

Today, the main entrance drive ends at a long grilled gate. Two short ramps lead to the terrace of the villa's forecourt. This section of the villa was added by Giovanni Ruggeri in 1730. Extending due north from the arcaded rear, a path leads through a four part parterre section, no longer planted, with a fountain at its center. To the left is the *limonaia* (greenhouse for lemon trees), whose roof is topped with paired stone putti between an eagle, lion, and coat of arms of the Arconati. There is also an aviary filled with chattering birds. Once, pots were filled with hibiscus and lemon trees; today, the enormous empty pots line the opposite low wall. On the side of the *limonaia* is the water tower which served as a reservoir for the numerous fountains and water tricks in the garden, such as the marble table which emitted a fine spray, soaking the unsuspecting visitors sitting around it.

Farther along the northern axis one passes the long hornbeam tunnel which cuts diagonally west-east across the garden. On the left is a small green theater surrounded by treillage. On the right is a portion of the woods. The northern axis terminates at an intersection of paths marked by fanciful herms. Here a circular clearing contains a round fountain ornamented with dragons. At the north end is an imposing archway framing a statue of Diana, goddess of the hunt. Six dogs are at her feet and nymphs recline in the flanking niches. The path to the left leads to the west gate of the park; to the right it passes

Left:
Topiary trees before the main façade

Below:
Mosaic steps leading up to the Perspective

through the woods along the northern wall, leading to the large aviary, now in ruins, but still salvageable. Halfway to the aviary a path bisects the route; a large round pool, dotted with water lilies, is visible through the woods. Once, a central jet gushed water over three hundred feet high. The marchioness, an invalid, often spent hours here, watching the patterns of light filtering through the trees onto the mirror surface of the water. It is a somewhat melancholy place, inhabited by pheasant, small hares, and a white rabbit. The woods were originally planted as complicated garden rooms, now replaced with simplified criss-crossing paths. The hornbeam tunnel leads to a croquet lawn in front of the east gate and, at the center, opens onto a clearing with four short corridors leading off it. Eight marble statues of the cardinal sins are set here in clipped-hedge niches. A gently tiered ramp is flanked by descending water channels fed by winged griffins. This leads to the vast lawn bisected by the carriage drive. In the past this was the great parterre, laid out in *broderie* (elaborate arabesque) bands. It still ends in a hemicycle before the imposing entrance gates. To the right of the lawn is a portion of the garden that has retained its lines according to the original plan. This is the garden of Hercules, dominated by a statue of Hercules and the Nemean lion. Beyond is an orchard, formerly planted with flowerbeds but soon to become a parking lot.

Located between Varese and Milan at Castellazzo di Bollate, the villa was a favored meeting place of the nobility during the summer and fall seasons. It was appreciated for its fine food and the quality of its musical entertainments.

The flat terrain and original *broderie* parterres gave the garden a

A fountain griffin

An allée being clipped

horizontal emphasis; this, combined with the treeless, sweeping vistas and creation of garden rooms, similar to those designed by André le Nôtre at Versailles, create a decidedly French atmosphere at Villa Arconati.

Castel Lebenberg

Cermes, Merano
Gardens open to the public

Formal gardens are rare in the Val d'Adige. Although the mountains surrounding Merano are studded with over thirty castles, only one has a noteworthy garden—and it is in miniature.

The Castel Lebenberg is beautifully sited, bathed in late afternoon sun above Cermes (or Tscherms). It was built as a defensive castle, but because it was not in a strategic location it was spared warfare and remains intact to this day. The original tower dates from 1260, built by the lords of Marlengo. From these counts the name Lebenberg or Monteleone derives, a corruption of the German *loewe*, after their family crest of a lion. The family of Marlengo died out in 1426; their castle was inherited in 1451 by the Fuchs von Fuchsenberg. The Fuchs were among the most powerful families in the region, counting among their relatives a number of archbishops. They also owned the Castel Giovo in Passaio, twelve miles from Castel Lebenberg, yet visible from the tower. On nights of festivities, they would

The rose garden within the castle walls

toast family members in the other castle by lighting bonfires. The castle was added to from the sixteenth century onward. The Fuchs held the castle until 1828. From 1835 until 1918 a Merano businessman named Kirchlechner owned the castle. In 1925 Abraham Adrian van Rossem van Sinoutskerke bought Castel Lebenberg. After heavy rains destroyed the stables, Van Rossem replaced them with the formal parterre in 1935. His son Jan now maintains the castle, its garden, and vineyards with great care.

The small, elegant parterre is divided into multiple compartments of box containing pink and white roses. Delicate water jets rise from small white marble basins. The parterre is bordered by box hedges and crenellated boundary walls that overlook the Merano valley. In the corner is a two-hundred-year-old mulberry tree. Ramps edged with hedges and punctuated by cypresses lead up to the castle walls. Almond trees, figs, and lilacs fill the outer courtyard. By the inner entrance is a trellis with wisteria growing up over the walls. Within is a charming sixteenth-century courtyard, lush with ivy and geraniums.

The sheltered courtyard of the castle

Villa Zambonina

Vigasio
Gardens may be open upon
request:
Signora Maria Cicogna Farina
Via Zambonina
Vigasio (Verona)

The parterre garden of Villa Zambonina is small and perfect—a dainty complement to the feminine character of the airy Baroque villa that stands beside it.

Set on a marshy plain, Zambonina began as an agricultural estate in 1653, a role it continues to this day in its production of rice and corn. Girolamo di Gasparo started with about one hundred fields, half planted with vineyards in the mid-seventeenth century. By 1683 he had doubled that land, concentrating on rice fields. The expanded property also contained a fortified fifteenth-century tower and convent. In 1706 a Baroque villa was built with three triple-arched loggias on the ground floor facing the garden. The Giusti family created the garden and commissioned the frescoes from the same artist who repeated his themes in their Verona palazzo. Early in this century the villa was bought by an industrialist, whose granddaughter, Maria Cicogna Farina, cares for it today.

The garden has been abandoned and then recreated over the years. Tall privet hedges enclose a parterre on three sides, creating a garden room closed on the fourth side by the villa itself. The long rectangular parterre has segmented, box-enclosed flowerbeds. The centers are of alternating circular or diamond shapes, filled with pink roses. Statues of the four seasons stand amid the roses. Beyond the hedge is a moat which runs alongside the road on two sides. At the side of the villa is a cutting garden with dahlias and roses next to a curving, vine-covered loggia surrounding a round swimming pool.

Pink roses fill the parterre of this feminine garden

Following:
A canal irrigates the fields around the Villa Zambonina. The formal garden lies hidden behind the hedges

Villa Trento da Schio

Costozza di Longare
Gardens may be open upon
request:
Conte Alvise da Schio
Villa Trento da Schio
Costozza di Longare (Vicenza)

Tucked against the Berici Hills are the ancient quarries of Costozza. Last used by Andrea Palladio in the late seventeenth century, they provided him with the white stone for his buildings in Vicenza. Three artificial grottoes mark these quarries. In recent years they have been used for cultivation of mushrooms, as a cantina for Vino Costozza da Schio, the wines grown on the slopes of the hills, and as a source of air conditioning for three nearby villas which were built by the Trento family. These stony hills were never rich in soil. Five narrow terraces were excavated on their slopes, originally to grow fruit for the table of the main Trento villa. Linked by staircases, these terraces form a perspective garden viewed from the road. The axis is not perfectly in line, and the height of the terraces vary, but the overall effect functions well.

The counts Morlini di Trento came to Costozza di Longare in the late fifteenth century. By the next century, they had established an agricultural estate of vineyards and orchards and gathered around them a literary circle with links to the Accademia in Vicenza. Contemporaries described a park covering three hills, with fish ponds, wild animals within an enclosure, aviaries, apple orchards, and a flower garden with topiary—all of which has vanished. A portion of a pavilion, known as the House of the Winds, is all that remains of this sixteenth-century park. In the archives of Venice is a drawing by Antonio Trecco for Ottavio Trento of the property as it existed in 1770; the terraces are faintly sketched in pencil.

The Villa Trento da Schio, originally called Villa Garzadora, was built around 1686 by Abbot Alberto Garzadori. The present owner, Count Alvise Trento da Schio, recently discovered terracotta drain pipes on one of the terrace levels, indicating that in Medieval times there was a house here. Above the villa is the Villino della Grotta, where the sculptor Orazio Marinali lived. The main villa lies on the plain beneath Villa Trento da Schio. In 1830 the estate passed to the da Schio family, and it remains in their hands today.

The grandfather of the current owner, also named Alvise, removed the greenhouses which stood on four levels, retaining only a portion of the uppermost *limonaia* (greenhouse for lemon trees). This

A statue of Venus in a rustic niche

is now incorporated into the villa as a sunroom. He planted a landscape garden with a *montagnola* (an artificial mount used as a belvedere) and laid out flowerbeds on the terraces.

The top terrace was planted with chestnut trees, but their roots gradually pushed out the sustaining walls and they were replaced with young lime trees. Flowerbeds are filled with orange lilies in June. They surround a central basin in which float waterlilies.

The second terrace has a grotto dating from the sixteenth century; today, the two rear chambers are open. In the center is a fountain statue of Neptune by Orazio Marinali. The statues in this garden are mostly by Marinali and his workshop, still standing in their original places; they form an unusual collection, for most of Marinali's production has been scattered with time. The statues, however, have been damaged by industrial smog. On the right is a small courtyard by the villa. In the flowerbeds are *saxifrage,* yucca, yellow iris, and lavender; pink roses grow against the villa. Pots contain agave. On the terrace itself, light blue iris with variegated leaves grow in beds. Purple clematis climbs over a door. Hydrangea blooms against a stone staircase leading to the glassed-in loggia with Ionic columns. On the stair railings are six dwarfs by Marinali of fine quality.

The third terrace has a statue of Venus set in a niche; water spurts from her breasts. The niche has a rock crystal set above the head of Venus and a fossil is incorporated into the base. Here, a box allée has replaced the old greenhouses. There is one replacement statue, substituting a piece toppled when the English occupied the villa during World War II.

The fourth terrace was originally a vegetable garden. When Count Alvise inherited the property in 1918, he extended the staircase by two steps, curving the final risers so that all the stairs would be visible upon entering the drive. The potatoes and beans were replaced with a grass tennis court, the net placed off center so as not to distract from the perspective.

Around 1820 Count Giovanni Trento planted the cypresses that cover the hilltop. There were once two palms facing the villa; the taller of the pair fell the day the present owner's eldest daughter died. Alongside the villa at second-story level is a wisteria-covered terrace, planted eighty-five years ago for the marriage of Count Alvise's parents.

Six dwarfs by Marinali
stand above the staircase
leading to the villa

This private garden is tended with much affection by the owners and is open to the public upon written application.

75 · *Villa Trento da Schio*

Villa Trissino

Trissino
Gardens may be open upon request:
Conte Giannino Marzotto
Piazza Trissino
Trissino (Vicenza)

Midway between Verona and Vicenza, at Trissino, a fortress stood on the ancient site of a Roman colony whose task it was to stem the flood of barbarians from over the Alps. The Trissino family built the Medieval fortress overlooking the sweeping valley of Agno and the surrounding hills of Montecchio and Arzignano. The garden is designed around these views. Its strategic importance was lost early in the fifteenth century when the Veneto came under Venetian domination, and centuries of peace ensued. With this change the fortress was transformed into a villa sometime before the seventeenth century. Its present form dates from the eighteenth century, when it lost the crenellations.

On a lower level of the site a second villa was erected, probably by another branch of the Trissino family, the Trissino Reale. Although it is undocumented, this villa most likely dates originally from the seventeenth century, but was twice devastated by fire. It now stands abandoned, a romantic ruin overlooking a vast octagonal basin set

The reflecting pool below the abandoned villa in the lower garden

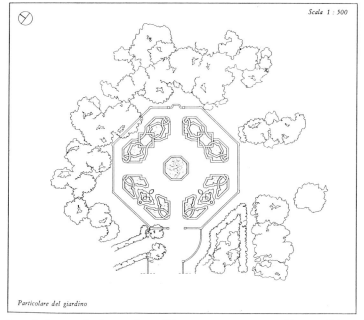

Scala 1 : 500

Particolare del giardino

in a balustraded meadow. The present owner, Count Giannino Marzotto, has asked for permission to rebuild it, but the Belle Arti balks when it comes to permitting transformation of interior structure—so it falls apart.

Both villas became the property of the Baston branches of the Trissinos in the eighteenth century. Alessandro Trissino Baston was the last of his line; when he died around 1850, he left the estate to his grandson, Antonio da Porto, son of Francesca Trissino. In 1949 Count Marzotto bought the property.

The garden is set in a park of fifty-seven acres and is composed of various sections joined by stairways. The layout is determined by the terrain of the hillside, with careful attention to the best view locations. The upper and lower villas do not face each other and appear to be independent entities. A romantic wood with meandering paths joins the two sections. This is a garden for strolling or horseback riding. By the castello is a raised, roughly triangular paddock, reached by ramps within the walls of the adjacent grassy courtyard. This is the highest point of the garden; one can climb its minaret to survey the valley and town below. Horses were exercised here under shifting clouds. Below it, along the cliff, is the citrus allée. This is reached from the front drive of the castello, through the fanciful pinnacled stone gates by Francesco Muttoni. A Latin plaque on the gates exhorts the visitor to admire the views of hills and plains, where art is a friend of nature.

As you walk down the lemon allée, the views southwest are impressive—the main road of Trissino borders the garden at this point.

Left: The upper gate by Francesco Muttoni

Above: Roses and hydrangea in the courtyard

The allée is at an angle to the upper villa or castello, and ends in an octagonal belvedere whose entrance is marked by two ancient cypresses. The citrus allée has a stone retaining wall on one side, bordered by hydrangeas. The opposite site of the broad path is open to the panorama of the village and hills beyond. The grassy octagonal belvedere is divided into four intricate, stone-bordered parterre segments set around a small central octagonal bed of red geraniums.

The castello's L-shaped plan embraces a vast courtyard. A harmonious structure of stone arches on three sides surrounds the lush lawn. Red cocktail roses swathe the walls. A curtain of cypresses is seen beyond the far wall, which conceals a small formal garden. Within the arches are large marble vases and statues. Earth was excavated to enlarge this courtyard and used to create the raised paddock area. In the courtyard a central *exedra* (an open-air niche), originally containing a fountain, now houses a badly battered car—a reminder of Count Giannino Marzotto's close escape from a racing accident. He twice won the arduous Mille Miglia road race.

The park is especially lovely in the fall when the foliage in the park glows with color and the Virginia creeper blazes. Roses bloom into mid-November. In 1987 an unusually heavy snowfall with lasting freezing temperatures damaged the laurel, jasmine, olive, and cypress trees. Among the thirty-nine important trees lost in a tornado with winds over sixty miles an hour were three large Maritime pines.

In the woods near the lower villa are various memorials to the Trissino family and also a pagan altar.

The lower villa is partially crenellated and overgrown with vines; weeds cover the twin flights of stairs to the large enclosed lawn below. A large octagonal reflecting pond dominates the meadow, and everywhere are wonderful statues, silent observers of the guests who chattered and roamed around this garden, leaning over the balconies to gaze on the vast valley below. These statues are among the finest in the Veneto. Many are vine clad and are now awaiting restoration. They come from the workshop of Orazio Marinali. None of them has his signature, but many can safely be attributed to his hand. The names of Giacomo Cassetti and Angelo Marinali have also been raised as possible sculptors of some of the statues on stylized bases. These represent figures in eighteenth-century dress and date from around 1715. Some characters are repeated, which leads to the assumption that they were made for various properties and later collected and transported here. Part of the romantic beauty of this lower villa is the state of gentle neglect that surrounds it. Count Marzotto envisions it as a site for ballet performances.

Within the upper villa is a fresco painted in 1793 for Andrea da Porta, showing the castello with crenellations, the terrace, and minaret, as well as the lower villa. The castello took its present form from a design by Girolamo dal Pozzo, who was in charge of the construction after the death of Francesco Muttoni. Following the idea of Mut-

The lemon garden with a view of the village of Trissino in the distance

toni, dal Pozzo enclosed the adjacent courtyard of the *cavalierizza*, or riding school.

The main outlines of the garden are the work of Francesco Muttoni. The linked allées, octagonal belvedere, large courtyard, and terraces along the old enclosing walls are his. His career was centered in the Veneto; he republished Palladio's writings between 1740 and 1747. A design project by Muttoni exists with colors denoting what pre-existed and notations of works to be carried out. He envisioned unusual parterre designs, basins, fountains, statues, ramps, and stairs—both concealed and in the open air. After Muttoni died in 1747, the garden plan was modified by Giovanni dall'Acqua. Muttoni's plans were not carried out for leveling the terraces by the citrus allée, the eastern area by the town street, nor the guard walkways.

The conscientious maintenance of the outer walls, nearly twenty feet high in places, the constant battle against spreading briars, and thoughtful replanting ensure that this garden, so intrinsically linked with its natural environment, survives for the pleasure of future generations.

Marble urns stand in the arches of the courtyard

Orto Botanico di Padova

*Padua
Gardens open to the public
(closed Saturdays and
Sunday afternoons)*

The world's oldest botanical garden is attached to the University of Padua; incredibly, it retains for the most part its original layout. Despite the passage of four centuries, the plan is still extremely functional.

The garden is compact. Besides the original round enclosure, it comprises a small arboretum and greenhouse area, covering a total of four and one half acres. It is tucked into a shady corner of Padua, off a side street bordered by a lush green canal, only steps away from the pilgrimage church of Sant'Antonio.

Early in the sixteenth century a botany or *semplici* department

Roses blooming within the old botanic garden; on the encircling wall are busts of botanists

was created in the University, the first such department in Europe, to instruct doctors on herbal healing properties. Professor Francesco Bonafede realized the necessity of having a living collection of such plants accessible to students. In 1545 the Orto Botanico was born under the auspices of the patrician amateur botanist Daniele Barbaro. The garden was planted under the direction of Professor Pietro da Nola, its design by architect Giovanni Moroni da Bergamo.

Outside the original walled garden is a section devoted to plants typically found in the Mediterranean

The circular garden was designed in four sections around a central fountain, enclosed by a tall brick wall, later surmounted by a white pietra d'Istria balustrade. Four entrances placed in the cardinal directions have large, wrought-iron gates.

Although there had long been privately assembled collections of plants, this was the first systematically gathered collection accessible to the public.

The garden is meticulously tended by a large squad of gardeners. When I visited, sun filtered through the trees in the arboretum as a group of school children who were being herded by their teacher through the garden lingered over carnivorous and sensitive plants outside one of the three greenhouses. The ticket seller sat peacefully with his young daughter in the shade of two magnolias planted in 1800.

The garden is set out in sections. Within the walled circle are areas for aquatic plants, useful plants for medicinal or industrial purposes, members of the grass family, irises, peonies, roses, ranunculus, ferns, and in summer a collection of cactus plants. Atop the walls, busts of botanists survey the plants below.

Against the wall to the right of the north gate is the famed Goethe palm planted in 1585, covered winters by its octagonal greenhouse since 1874. A plaque relates how Johann Wolfgang von Goethe visited the garden in 1787 and formulated his theory of the morphology of plants—that all plant forms derive from one original plant.

The aquatic plant section favorably impressed the French geographer Charles de Brosses in 1739, who compared the garden to the botanical garden in Paris and noted its lack of aquatic plants (however, he did find Padua's greenhouse inferior). The proximity of the thermal baths of Albano ensure a constant warm temperature in the aquatic plant tanks.

Beyond the enclosure is a small arboretum including an oriental plane tree planted in 1680, and an enormous, fossilized oak trunk found in Padua, carbon-dated to at least twenty-six hundred years ago.

Opposite the greenhouses is a fascinating collection representing plants first introduced to Europe from this botanical garden. Among them are the sunflower, potato, lilac, black walnut, locust tree, sesame, rhubarb, Virginia creeper, morning glory, and sourgum.

The rules of the garden set in 1545 are inscribed on marble tablets placed on the entrance gates. Written in Italian and Latin, the regulations are still valid, although the punishments are undoubtedly not as severe, and the visiting hours have changed:

1. Do not knock on this door before the day of St. Mark Evangelist (April 25), nor before 10 A.M.
2. He who enters for study is not to wander beyond the circular wall.
3. In the garden it is forbidden to break stems or branches, pull out flowers, gather seeds or fruit, to lay roots bare.

4. It is forbidden to crush small plants and also to trample or walk on the beds.

5. In no other way shall the garden be damaged.

6. Nothing is to be done against the will of the director.

7. The transgressor will be punished with fines, prison and exile.

De Brosses was attracted to another inscription on the gate pilaster: "hic oculi, hinc manus," meaning "Here one looks with the eyes, not the hands."

A plan of the original layout from Places of the Past, *1980*

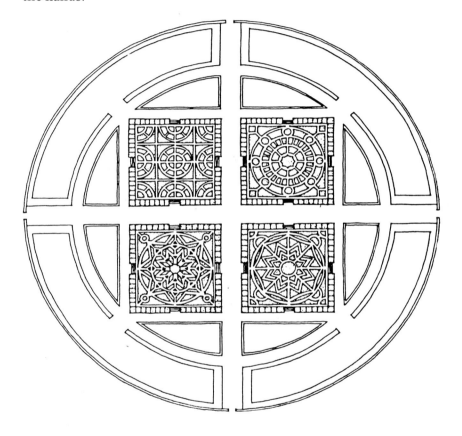

Villa Emo Capodilista

Rivella di Monselice
Gardens closed to the public

One of the loveliest gardens in Italy is that of Villa Emo Capodilista. It partially recreates a pre-existent, eighteenth-century garden on the site, borrowing from traditional Veneto gardens, as well as English flower borders and landscape parks. The Brenta Canal borders the front of the property; as a result, the earth is particularly fertile. The gardens cover eighteen level acres adjacent to cultivated fields. The Euganean Hills can be seen in the far distance.

Villa Emo Capodilista has remained in the same family since it was designed in 1588 by Vincenzo Scamozzi. An old plan of the estate from the seventeenth century shows the entrance by the Brenta and the villa flanked on both sides by long, narrow fishponds. These fish ponds were rediscovered in 1966 when Countess Giuseppina Emo designed the present garden. From the balcony of the villa one looks down on the entrance parterre of box that spells out the interlaced initials of Andrea Emo and his wife Giuseppina Pignatelli. This boxwood lettering is an old Renaissance conceit; another preserved example is found at Villa Ruspoli near Viterbo. At first the parterre at Villa Emo was planted with flowers, but this proved impractical and brown gravel from Verona now covers the patches between the clipped box. In the center is a low round fountain basin with a small seventeenth-century statue. When the gate bell is rung, the owner's two large Maremma sheepdogs come running across the parterre as if it were a steeplechase course.

Long broad bands of rosebeds face the parterre on the sides. Parallel to them, at a slightly lower level, are the restored fishponds. The ponds are now filled with waterlilies and Calla lilies, purple loosestrife, iris, and lavender grow on the banks according to the season. The property line facing the villa is marked by a row of tall poplars. Chinese iris is tucked into a shady corner. Yucca grows against the gates, setting off the villa and farm house from the rear garden. Pink roses border the fishponds and two large rectangular beds of red and white roses stand next to the side of the villa. Five thousand rose bushes bloom continuously for a six-month period. The white roses were introduced in the mid-1980s. These swaths of roses are an unforgettable sight.

87 · *Villa Emo Capodilista*

The initials of the owners
in boxwood are legible
from the balcony

An English landscape garden is located to the left of the villa. At
the end of the poplar allée stands a statue of a warrior, marking the
limit of the garden. A path leads past a willow tree and a Japanese
maple at the edge of a small pond. An allée of magnolias and pomegranates, lined with rows of irises, leads back to the villa. It borders an
apple orchard concealing a swimming pool.

A gravel court with an old wellhead sets off the large rear garden.
Shoulder-high privet hedges surround a lawn with a filled-in, rectan-

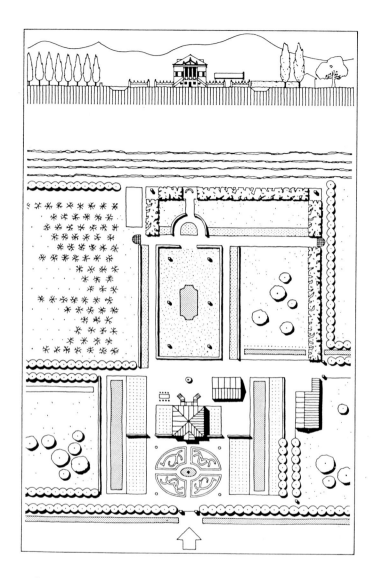

gular pool in the middle. On two sides of the garden are long perennial beds in the English manner. A stunning collection of primulas, carnations, monks-hoods, peonies, lupins, poppies, lavender, lamb's ears, columbine, and phlox blend colors in the side beds. At the far end, irises and lilies flank a small rose bed on axis with the filled-in pool, wellhead, and villa staircase. The entire rear garden is surrounded by a curving tunnel of hornbeam broken by wisteria and white rose-covered arbors. The hornbeam tunnel is a traditional feature of Veneto gardens.

Countess Marina Emo Capodilista has inherited her mother's enthusiasm and love for the garden.

Castello del Cataio

Battaglia Terme
Gardens may be open upon
request:
Castello del Cataio
Battaglia Terme (Padova)

The large courtyard of Cataio was once flooded for naumachia—*or mock sea battles*

The Castello del Cataio at Battaglia Terme is an imposing fortress set on the edge of the Brenta Canal. Its gardens weave in and out of the massive structure, originally built by Beatrice Pia degli Obizzi as a villa in the sixteenth century. Her son Pio Enea I was a military commander in the service of the Venetian Republic. Between the years 1570 and 1573 he hired the architect Andrea della Valle to add to the villa and transform it into a fortress with drawbridge, crenellations, and room enough to house his garrison. A portion of the land to the west was designated a hunting preserve. His grandson, Marquis Pio Enea II, inherited the property in 1648. With great zeal and at great expense he rebuilt the castello over eighteen years, adding to and transforming it. The gardens are largely his creation. The Obizzi line ended with Tommaso in 1803. He was a collector of antiquities, coins, arms, and armor, and possessed the Gonzaga collection of musical instruments. At his behest, the entire property went at his death to the Duke of Modena. The castello and grounds subsequently passed to the Hapsburg family. Archduke Franz Ferdinand used it as a summer residence, adding a large wing to the north. A special railway track was laid across the plain to the west, facilitating Hapsburg visits and the transport of Tommaso degli Obizzi's collections to Vienna. Now the castello is owned by the heirs of the della Francesca family.

Our knowledge of the garden outside the castle walls derives from a description of the property made in 1669 by the Italian satirist Francesco Berni after Pio Enea II's improvements. Included in *Descrizione del Cataio* (Berni, 1669) is an engraving showing the outer garden in construction. Berni tells of four large heraldic arms in box, depicting the emblems of the Medici, Este, Republic of Venice, and the Vatican (the *palle* or balls, an eagle, a lion, and the keys of Saint Peter). Pio Enea held estates in each of these territories. Two large identical fishponds had columned structures with cupolas covered in jasmine and clematis. Today, the fishpond to the west remains, but the cypresses that used to stand at the corners of the ponds have gone. The other fishpond was filled in and planted with trees. A willow and magnolias bordering the remaining pool were added in the eighteenth century. Tunnels of hornbeam trace the central path. Pio Enea

The castle from the canal

II raised the main road to run parallel to the castle. The exterior castle wall in the garden is terraced; roses, wisteria, and hydrangea grow against it. Lemons were featured on the Obizzi family coat of arms, and in the time of Pio Enea II there were a great many potted citrus plants in this garden, on walls, between crenellations, and on the castle terraces. Recently, however, the vast greenhouses that sheltered these plants were destroyed by fire.

Within the castle is a labyrinth of levels and courtyards. At ground level is a vast rectangular courtyard. Here tournaments and *naumachia*, theatrical sea battles, were held. The courtyard is closed by a wing that housed a theater built for Pio Enea II. Steps lead up to a much smaller courtyard with a fanciful grotto filled with carved figures of Bacchus on his barrel, satyrs, putti with baskets of flowers, the four winds, and an elephant. Nearby, flanking a staircase, are statues of two river gods set in grotto niches with basins below. Once the coral necklace of one squirted water at those who approached too closely. There was also once an aviary in this so-called Courtyard of the Giants. Besides containing a large variety of live birds, it had a marble eagle fountain with water issuing from its beak.

Climbing to the next level one passes by a statue of Cerberus, guard dog of Hades. Water flows from his three mouths. The castello abounds in cryptic inscriptions linked to its sculpture; the base of Cerberus reads "Papè Satan Aleppe." Sculpted in high-relief on the reverse of the Bacchus grotto below is a head of Medusa.

The roof of the original villa was remade as a large terrace. From here can be viewed the network of courtyards and surrounding countryside. A fountain of Janus, with water descending from a shell into an eight-lobed pool stands on this terrace.

Seen from the terrace is a walled garden below. At present it is overgrown, yet there are still box parterre patterns and ancient cypresses. Originally, it was divided into three compartments of box parterres with cypresses at the corners. The two lateral compartments each had a central marble fountain intertwined with overgrown cypresses, so that the water seemed to issue forth from the branches and fall into the pools beneath. A loggia overlooks this garden, and contains a fountain of the seven-headed Hydra, spewing forth water rather than flames. At its foot is a toad, which spits water at the visitor.

At present the gardens are not in pristine condition. The owners have plans to open the castle and restore the gardens gradually.

The grotto of Bacchus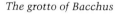

Villa Verità
Il Boschetto

San Pietro di Lavagno
Gardens may be open upon
request:
Signor Domenico Fraccaroli
Villa Verità
San Pietro di Lavagno (Verona)

*The fountain statue of
Hercules and Anteus by
Girolamo Campagna*

Beyond Verona, in the hills of San Briccio is the Villa Verità, once
home to the poet Gerolamo Verità. The site he chose is on a steep,
woody hillside overlooking fields; hence it also became known as Il
Boschetto—or little woods. In ancient Roman days this was the location of a villa, traces of which remain adjacent to the present structure. Undoubtedly, this legacy appealed to Verità, the humanist.

In 1553, the year following his death, an inventory of the property was drawn up listing 136 fields surrounding the villa. By 1683
the number of fields had grown to 348. The principal crops were olives, grapes, and mulberries. It remains an agricultural property to
this day.

The garden itself was made for a later Gerolamo Verità around
the turn of the seventeenth century. The statue of Hercules and Anteus, on which the garden axis pivots, was sculpted by the Venetian
Girolamo Campagna around 1595. Based on an inscription over the
grotto, the garden was probably completed by 1616. Both Michele
San Micheli and Domenico Curtoni have been proposed as architects
of the villa and garden. The villa was much rebuilt in the eighteenth
century. The existence of a detailed design by Alessandro Pompei
in the Uffizi, showing both villa and garden, would indicate that he
bid for the job.

The main hall of the villa opens into the middle level, or hanging
garden, which extends over a vast rectangular terrace built against
the hillside. In the best Italian garden tradition, this is a true axial
garden linked to the villa. The central pool's fountain figure of Hercules marks the cross axis of the line from the villa and the ascent of
the hillside. The garden comprises three levels linked by sets of monumental stairways, a scheme very possibly derived from the courtyard of the Belvedere in the Vatican and hence from the ancient
Temple of Fortune at Palestrina. The middle level can be likened to a
vast *salotto*, or living room, an extension of the villa itself. From
Bartolomeo Clesio's property drawing of 1742, we see the garden
much as it appears today. This hanging garden was drawn with three
shaped basins; today there is only the center one. This basin has an
elegant contour marked by a stone balustrade. The choice of Hercules

*Right:
A riot of color provided
by dahlias, salvia, and
roses*

95 · *Villa Verità* · *Il Boschetto*

A carving of a swimming man appears in the water channel of a handrail

as a garden figure was a popular one, as he served as an allusion to the garden of Hesperides in which there was a tree of golden apples that Hercules had to gather for his twelfth labor. Stretches of lush lawn are bordered by parterres of red and orange dahlias and salvia. Rosemary, hydrangea, and roses grow here too. Within the retaining wall is part of the aqueduct, a trough in one long piece of stone. A request was made of the authorities in 1596 to divert water from the small Dugale River in the town of Mezzane for use by the villa. From here the water supplies the fountains, and then descends beneath the terrace into the grotto.

Ascending the black-and-white pebbled steps from the hanging garden terrace, one passes two antique Roman statues. At the top is a grassy clearing, mysteriously labeled "La Rena," or sand, on Clesio's property map. Against the overgrown hillside one can make out traces of an amphitheater destroyed in an earthquake sometime before the seventeenth century. Gerolamo Verità and his father Michele were both theater enthusiasts and members of the Accademia Filarmonica in the late sixteenth century.

Once again on the middle level is a balustrade set with mannerist masks. From here is a view of the pond below. Flights of stairs descend to the lower garden level. The handrails are channelled for water to trickle down their carved surfaces. Low stone carvings of lilies, masks, shells, a dolphin, a salamander, a turtle, a serpent eating a frog, birds, a man stretched out as if to sunbathe, and a woman emerge in the light from among the lichen.

Between the steps is a large grotto, faced with large blocks of cut stone. Within the spacious rectangular room are three tiered fountains set into pillared niches. In front of the grotto is a fourteenth-century wellhead in wrought iron. The lake is surrounded by thick vegetation. Clesio showed it as a rectangle with scalloped edges, which have since been straightened out.

Emerging from the water is a modern interpretation of the Maid of Copenhagen, placed there by the current owner. On the left towards the villa are traces of the ancient Roman building, interspersed with modern sculpture and a nineteenth-century quartet of dwarfs. The forecourt, approached by a sloping drive, is fragrant with potted bergamint, oranges, and lemons. Near the chapel is a statue of Saint Anthony with his pig.

Villa Verità remained in the Verità family until the middle of the eighteenth century. The last heir married Count Montanari and the property passed into his family. Early in this century the Grassi family sold it to the father of the present owner, Domenico Fraccaroli. The gardens are very much alive today. Besides hosting the raucous activities of twenty-two grandchildren, the gardens have been used in recent years for concerts of the Chigiana di Siena, fashion shows for Giorgio Armani and Krizia, as well as the launching of Indro Montanelli's *Il Giornale di Milano*.

II *Tuscany*
Marche

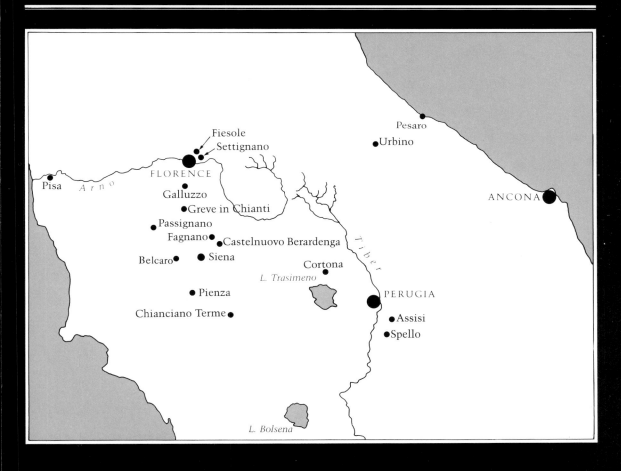

Fiesole
Settignano
FLORENCE
Pisa   *Arno*
Galluzzo
Greve in Chianti
Passignano
Fagnano
Castelnuovo Berardenga
Belcaro
Siena
Pienza
Chianciano Terme
Cortona
L. Trasimeno
Tiber
PERUGIA
Assisi
Spello
Pesaro
Urbino
ANCONA
L. Bolsena

Orto Botanico di Pisa

Pisa
Gardens open to the public on
weekdays

The Botanic Institute
building

Patronized by the Grand Dukes of Tuscany, the Orto Botanico of Pisa
was founded as part of the University of Pisa in 1543. Since its creation it has moved twice within the city, starting out near the westerly
stretch of the Arno at the Citadella. It was known then as the Orto
Botanico alle Stallette and as the Medici Garden of the Arsenal. It
expanded in 1563 next to the former convent of Santa Marta in Via
del Giardino near Galileo's birthplace, and finally in 1595 it was con-
solidated and moved to its present location between Via Roma and
Via Santa Maria, adjacent to the university.

Its decorative layout seen in the plan of 1723 has regrettably vanished, the parterres reduced in 1866 and 1877 to simple rows broken
by the old round basins, the arched arbors only a memory. However,
traces remain in the old entrance gate and the rusticated Botanic Institute building. The actual extent of the garden has been more than
doubled to the north.

The founder, Luca Ghini, also was responsible for the creation of
the Botanical Garden of Florence in 1544. He taught medicine in
Pisa from 1543 to 1554. Ghini was tremendously influential in the
development of botanical studies. He abandoned the antique method
of plant commentary in favor of direct observation. He was possibly
the first to dry plants for study, forming a herbarium. His pupil and
successor as director was Andrea Cesalpino, who was the first to
classify plants on a biological basis divided between "erbe"—herbs—
and "alberi"—trees. These were subdivided according to their production of seeds and fruit in his book *De plantis*, published in 1583.
His concept of genus was taken into consideration by Joseph Pitton de
Tournefort, John Ray, and Linnaeus—the Swedish botanist who developed the modern system of botanical nomenclature. Cesalpino
eventually left the garden to serve as physician to Pope Clement VIII.

Today the entrance is through Via Ghini. Originally it was from
Via Roma at the southwest corner of the garden. The iron gates remain, set in a frame of sixteenth-century mosaic with floral motifs.
The old Botanical Institute has a decorative pebble-and-shell-
encrusted façade with roses growing up its walls. It was built between
1591 and 1595 by Giuseppe Benincasa. Adjacent to the old Institute

is the Orto del Cedro—the Cedar Garden. *Cedro* in Italian also means citrus, but this section was named for an enormous Cedar of Lebanon that once grew in the garden.

A grove of bamboo separates the Cedar Garden from the Orto dei Semplici. The Simples Garden is surrounded by low, tiered walls on which pots containing medicinal herbs are set. It must be remembered that in the Renaissance medicine and botany were taught by the same professor. Students of medicine were expected to know the healing properties of plants. Botanical gardens began in Italy with this premise; only later were other nonmedicinal plants collected.

To the left of the Simples Garden is the banana greenhouse—an early example of an iron-glass house in Italy. Within grow orchids and ferns.

The extent of the early botanical garden was reduced by building the Museum of Natural History to the south. In 1841 the garden was enlarged to the north. This area, the Orto Nuovo, or New Garden, is partially an experimental zone, partly an arboretum.

In the northwest corner is a small lotus pond. An artificial *montagnola,* or hillock, is the setting for rock garden plants. Looking up, one is startled by the proximity of the Leaning Tower, glimpsed between trees beyond the garden wall.

A plan of the garden by Michelangelo Tilli, 1723

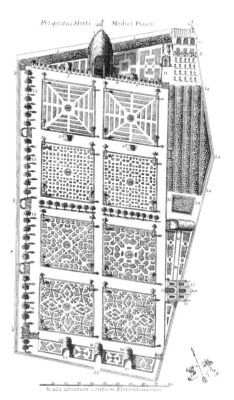

Prospectus Horti   Medici Pisani

Scala ulnarum centum Florentinarum

Villa i Tatti

Settignano
Gardens open upon request:
Villa i Tatti, Harvard
University
Via di Vincigliata 26
Settignano (Florence)

The green garden at Villa i Tatti is a twentieth-century creation, designed by an Englishman, yet it deserves a place among Italy's Classic gardens. It has a two-fold fascination: the garden itself, which descends gently down the slopes of Settignano, surrounded by the Arno River valley, and its place in the study of art history.

Bernard Berenson envisioned a utopian, isolated setting, Altamura, where scholars would live and share their ideas on aesthetics. Each month of the year would be focused on a specific topic, pertaining to "life in its beauty and essence." He published his monastic plan, based on Walter Pater's aesthetic ideals, in 1898. Not until 1905, when he was hired by Lord Duveen, was he able to realize his vision, purchasing the farm house I Tatti. Two English architects were called in, Geoffrey Scott and Cecil Pinsent. Scott was responsible for the renovations of the villa, until Berenson's wife, Mary Costelloe, fell in love with him. Berenson kept Scott on as his private secretary, but spitefully denied his participation in the redesigning of the villa. Cecil Pinsent designed the gardens, beginning planting the year after the property was acquired. He studied the gardens of the Italian Renaissance, and tried to recreate their flavor. Occasionally a tell-tale slip of his English heritage would appear, such as the pyramidal clipping of the green garden.

"I Tatti" is a corruption of Zatti, the name of the family who owned the farm house in 1563. When Berenson acquired it there was only an orchard. From Ponte a Mensola the road winds uphill alongside a torrent to the gates of the villa. Within is a small courtyard and a small eighteenth-century chapel. A long cypress allée runs parallel to the outside road and leads to the foot of the garden. From the other side of the villa, beyond the entrance to the library, is a small formal parterre garden.

As in traditional Tuscan villas, a terrace sets the house off from the garden. From here Berenson watched gunfire over Florence, July 31, 1944. Soon after, he went into hiding in the villa of the Serlupi family in nearby Fiesole; his wife Mary, an invalid, remained behind at I Tatti. Although the Germans did not occupy the villa, a certain amount of damage was done to the gardens.

Following:
Recently restored flowerbeds in a knot design on the villa's terrace

Beyond the terrace are two parterre beds in diamond shapes filled with begonias, asparagus ferns, pink cascading geraniums, and potted lemons. Steps descend into an airy cool greenhouse used as a summer room. Twin flights of steps curve down from there into the green garden, and then below to a sunken garden. The entire garden is enclosed by high hedges. Steps on an axis with the house divide the garden down the center. Each level is enclosed by low hedges, clipped in pyramidal shape. At the bottom, the sunken terrace has continuous stone benches around its edges, the center broken by a balcony overlooking the woods below. This terrace has two large flowerbeds planted with hyacinths, tulips, wild pinks, and narcissus. Straight twin flights of stairs take the visitor into an ilex *quincunx,* or a planting of trees in opposing rows, a meandering stepping stone path under its branches. Just beyond is the ancient church of San Martino.

Berenson died in 1959 at the age of 94, leaving the property of I Tatti, its library, and art collection to Harvard University. It is now the Harvard University Center for Italian Renaissance Studies, sustained by an endowment and the produce of the seventy-five acres of farms. The gardens are currently being restored by a fund set up by Lila Acheson Wallace.

It is possible to visit the garden upon written application.

Villa Peyron
Bosco di Fonte Lucente

Fiesole
Gardens open upon request:
Dottor Paolo Peyron
Via di Vincigliata 2
Fiesole (Florence)

The existence of the garden of Bosco di Fonte Lucente is entirely thanks to the devotion of Dr. Paolo Peyron, the last of the family that has owned the property since the beginning of this century. After massive destruction in the Second World War, he carefully restored the old garden and made yearly additions to it. Only recently has the garden become somewhat accessible to visitors. Peyron plans to leave the garden to the Fondo Ambiente Italiano to ensure its preservation for the future.

The villa is nestled on a hillside between Fiesole and Settignano, surrounded by woods and wildlife typical of this region. Through the trees a view of Florence is seen in the distance.

The first settlers here were Etruscans; traces of their habitation appear in the wall by the pond, as well as in the foundations of the villa itself. During the Renaissance, a patrician family from Pistoia, the Biagini, built the original villa, which was radically rebuilt early in this century.

An eighteenth-century engraving of Villa Peyron showing the entrance carriage ramp

Left:
The stairway leading down to the pond and olive groves

The sloping parterre beneath wisteria-covered walls

The "cloister garden" and chapel

Comparing the garden to a late eighteenth-century print, it is possible to see that the terrace level below the villa has been faithfully maintained. The sloping, uneven terrain is divided into a succession of terraces, linked by ramps and elegant staircases. The main axis of the garden is off-center to the villa; indeed, it borders the parterre set in its forecourt. A long ramp, edged with scalloped hedges, divides the second terrace. From the print it can be surmised that the original entrance to the villa was via this ramp, which would have been used as a carriage drive. The ramp's axis continues down to another sloping level with a parterre. The high cypress trees that border

A putto on a stair railing

it guide the eye across a large fishpond to a balcony, and then beyond to another railing on a lower level.

During World War II the villa was occupied by German Field Marshal Albert Kesselring and then by the S.S. The garden was shelled every six feet by Allied gunfire—and then taken over by English troops who moved into the villa and used one of the parterres as a turn-around for their trucks. Despite the battering they suffered, most of the box borders eventually reappeared. Much of the garden's terracotta statuary, however, was destroyed during the war.

Shortly after the war, Peyron had a phone call from a friend in the Veneto who informed him of a large cache of marble statues, culled from destroyed Venetian villas. The price of this treasure was basically the cost of hauling them away. Dr. Peyron did not hesitate, and the statues now enhance these gardens. There is also a set of marvellous Baroque male statues, bought from the estate of a mysteriously vanished Swedish industrialist.

The uppermost terrace by the house has a four-part parterre of low, double-box borders planted with roses. A wellhead stands in the center. The wall overlooking the descending terraces is decorated with a set of life-size statues. A fountain with Neptune is set against the wall of the villa. Lemons, sweet orange trees, bougainvillea, and gardenias are in pots. Hydrangeas line the far wall.

Down the ramp are two parterres; the one at the left is one of the original ones, reached by a small staircase from the *bosco*—or woods. The garden is reminiscent of a cloister, with a small stone chapel and arcade. The north wall of the ramp is covered with an ancient wisteria which blooms in June. The next terrace down is edged by tall cypresses. Dr. Peyron's father allowed the trees to grow naturally, but they are now clipped to keep open the view. A central box pattern with rounded, clipped bushes covers the slope down to the wide, balustraded reflecting pool.

Farther along is a marble rotonda, its bench surrounding a small fountain. Originally, there was a table in its place. Birds and grapes are carved on the columns, baskets of fruit on its curving lintel. These woods create a safe haven for animals who flock here for a rare source of water in Fiesole. Nightingales sing at dusk, mingling their song with the sounds of the fountains which are the soul of this garden. The path continues through the woods to a small Japanese lake with a little wooden bridge. In the spring bright yellow broom plants perfume these walks. A path leads around to the reservoir, set against the rising hills planted with olives. A swan named Teo, with companion ducks, swims on this small lake.

The property, including the olive groves, totals about one hundred acres; nearly ten of these comprise the well-tended garden. The spring is the only source of water for the twenty-eight fountains that give life to this garden set in the woods of Fiesole—hence its name Bosco di Fonte Lucente.

Villa Capponi

Florence
Gardens closed to the public

One of the most enchanting gardens in Italy, Villa Capponi can be likened to a jewel box. Within scalloped walls are three tiers of secret gardens, each with brilliant flowers embedded in green box compartments. The effect is intimate; indeed, visitors are not encouraged in this most private of gardens. Besides its beauty, it has great importance as an example of a small, late-Renaissance garden, believed to retain its original form. Old prints or plans of the garden regrettably are nonexistent, but there are no indications of major transformations. The garden was expanded in the nineteenth and twentieth centuries, and an access stairway was built into the lower secret garden. Yet the panoramic terrace, the walls enclosing the garden, and probably the expanse of lawn adjacent to the north façade are original, dating from the last quarter of the sixteenth century.

In 1572 a wealthy merchant, Gino di Lodovico Capponi, bought the property with a small house from bankrupt Niccolo Del Nero. Capponi transformed the house into a luxurious villa, and in all probability laid out the garden terraces. The Capponi held the property until 1882 when it was sold to the daughter of the duke of Portland, Mrs. Scott. She added the loggias, the staircase down to the secret garden (hitherto accessible only by a tunnel from the basement of the villa), and expanded the garden westward with another garden

Plan of Villa Capponi from Mader, Giardini all'italiana, *1987*

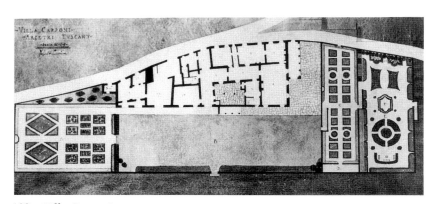

Following:
The secret garden is filled with lychnis in the spring, white impatiens in summer, and dahlias in the fall

*Florence can be seen in
the distance from the
garden of Villa Capponi*

room leading off the secret garden. In 1892, Lady Ottoline Morrell
came here to visit Mrs. Scott (the two women were related by marriage); she was undoubtedly influenced by Villa Capponi when it
came time to design her own gardens at Garsington, near Oxford.
"When I was convalescent," she wrote in her memoirs,

> I was invited by my aunt, Mrs. Scott, to go and stay with her at the Villa
> Capponi just outside the town, and there I spent an enchanted
> fortnight. . . . The Villa Capponi was a large old untouched Medici villa,
> standing high up at Arcetri, tier upon tier of terraces with walls covered
> with roses and sweet-scented flowers. Underneath lay Florence, the great
> bell of the Duomo leading the ding-dong chorus of clamour as Angelus
> floated up every evening (*Memoirs of Lady Ottoline Morrell: A Study in
> Friendship 1873–1915*, 1964).

This was not, in fact, a Medici villa, but Lady Ottoline's description
is still accurate. One of the greatest assets of the villa is indeed its
site, set in olive groves, with views of Florence from its terrace.

In 1928 Villa Capponi was sold to Mr. and Mrs. Henry Clifford.
The following year they had Cecil Pinsent design an extension of the
garden with a swimming pool. Since 1979 it has been owned by the
Benedetti family, who carefully maintain it. In 1987 Queen Elizabeth
made a nostalgic visit, recalling one she made as a child to Mrs. Scott.
Recently the garden appeared in a mystery, *Menacing Groves*, by John
Sherwood.

The villa is set at the junction of the Pian de' Giullari and Via
Vincenzo Viviani, in the southern zone above Florence known as Ar-
cetri. Though only ten minutes from the Ponte Vecchio, the property
is surrounded by countryside, and from the road there is no hint of
the garden within. Passing through the main entrance hall of the
villa, one emerges onto a lush rectangular lawn, faced by a wall covered with roses and trumpet vines. At the base of this northern garden
wall are peonies and beds planted with pansies in the spring and salvia in the fall. A great lime tree shades the lawn. On the garden façade
of the house grows an ancient wisteria that blooms in May. At the
western edge of the lawn is a loggia and terrace that provide vistas of
the surrounding hills and Florence in the distance. Here are pots of
perfumed jasmine, red hibiscus, and geraniums in the summer. A low
stone wall conceals the existence of the secret garden. Leaning over
the wall one discovers a sunny parterre fifteen feet below. From the
terrace is a staircase hugging the retaining wall. Wrought-iron gates
block the entrance to the tunnel, which in the past was the only access point to this garden. The Baroque scalloped walls are not typical
of Florence. The long narrow garden is totally taken up with two
rows of box-edged compartments designed in variations of rectangles.
These are filled in the spring with pink lychnis, in summer with
white impatiens, and dahlias in the fall.

In the center of the west wall, a gate leads to a second lower gar-

den room, reached by a flight of steps. Added late in the nineteenth century, it is larger than the preceding garden. This too has formal box-edged beds, but these are filled with enormous terracotta pots planted with blue plumbago. There is a lily pool in the center of the garden, and a high ∪-shaped yew hedge providing a sheltered place to sit. Flowerbeds flank the walls. These are filled with marigolds in the spring, red zinnias in the summer, and chrysanthemums, dahlias, and pink lilies in the fall.

A third garden room completes this end of the garden. Pinsent designed a rectangular swimming pool surrounded by clipped cypress walls. From here a path leads out into the olive groves, alongside the garden walls, past a cutting garden, greenhouse, and woods, back to the eastern end of the villa. Here is one more formal box parterre, guarded by griffins atop enclosing walls. A grilled window in the far wall gives a view of the tight compact design of box compartments, intended to be viewed as mats of color. Half the garden is designed in diamond or triangular shapes, the other half in rows of small rectangles. These are filled in spring with bright blue forget-me-nots, which contrast with the yellow lemon trees. Later on, ageratum continues the complementary blue-yellow color scheme.

This garden, unlike many Classic Italian gardens, depends for its effect not merely upon massing of evergreens, but upon the contrast of the colors of the flowers. Great attention is given at Villa Capponi to just the right shades of flowering material. One of the three gardeners is employed full time and has worked in this garden for thirty years. This continuity of care is the hallmark of Villa Capponi's garden.

Villa Agape

Florence
Gardens open upon request:
Villa Agape
Via Torre del Gallo 8
Florence

Via Torre del Gallo winds upward from the panoramic Viale dei Colli above Florence. Moments away from city traffic you find yourself in the countryside. Behind the old walls along the street are olive groves and gracious ancient villas where it is easy to imagine life continuing at a leisurely pace, as it did before World War I.

Behind the gates at number eight is such a villa. It has been through many transformations and now operates as a pensione run by the Suore Stabilite nella Carità. The villa's history dates back to 1472. At that time it was a large farm house which was sold to the nuns of San Paolo a Pinti by Maestro Bartolomeo di Matteo. In the mid-sixteenth century it was owned by Jacopo di Raffaello Del Nente, whose family sold it in 1602 to Giulio di Filippo Arrighetti. The basic form of the villa dates from his ownership. In the mid-nineteenth century the last of the Arrighettis sold the property to the Nestis.

Before World War I the villa was enlarged and a large loggia was built on the third story, with wonderful views of the hills surrounding Florence. In 1952 Duchess Anna of Aosta bought the villa and created the present garden from olive groves. She gave the property to the Suore Stabilite nella Carità, who have renamed it Villa Agape. The gardens are carefully tended under the nuns' supervision.

Villa Agape's gardens are terraced and varied in character. True to Classical Italian garden design, the main elements are drawn on a central axis from the rear entrance of the villa. A double-flight of steps leads down to a graveled terrace with a wellhead in its center. Below is a second courtyard with rippling sustaining walls and two raised formal parterre gardens. In front of the sunken court, continuing on a direct axis, is a stately cypress allée, which cuts through the sloping fields.

Adjacent to the villa on the right is a lawn with a small fountain. This is overlooked by a small, triple-arched loggia with a tiny chapel set into it at an angle. This area is set off from the rest of the garden by a wall pierced with arches, creating the mood of a cloister.

Below the wall is a path bordered on one side by ageratum, the other by pink begonias. This path curves gently upward, following the eighteenth-century-style, low-dipping wall of a small formal garden.

Following:
The salvia garden shimmering in the summer heat

Quartered, enclosed box beds are ablaze with red salvia. In the center is a lily pool. Small statues of lions guard the entrances into this garden.

The path winds up to a loggia banked with hydrangea, and farther up to a terrace at the edge of the property. Beyond the terrace a cut cypress hedge and low, ivy-covered wall separate the gardens from the fields. An informal rose garden follows the slope down to the area of the sunken formal garden. On the other side of the house, level with it, is a small garden composed of square-shaped beds. These are filled with marigolds and pink begonias. The overall effect is extremely pretty yet fragmented. Its appeal is greatly due to the surrounding countryside and views of Florence which enhance but do not dominate the garden.

The sunken garden

A view towards the villa
showing the slightly re-
cessed salvia garden

Villa la Bugia

Florence
Gardens may be open upon
request:
Contessa d'Entreves
Via Santa Margherita a
Montici
Florence

The front door of Villa la Bugia offers a glimpse of the garden beyond

When the main door opens at La Bugia one looks through a loggia, then through another opening with heavy blue-green wooden doors to the terrace garden beyond. The Valle dell'Ema, its hills south of Florence, unfolds in the distance. Only when you walk out onto the terrace itself are you aware of the highway in the valley below.

The design of La Bugia's garden has been slightly altered by the shifting of roads—the original country lane of Via Santa Margherita a Montici passed between the villa's original façade and the formal terrace garden. The garden was linked to the villa by a small bridge. In the 1870s, when Florence was capital of Italy, the road was moved.

Below:
The hanging garden of the villa

Its former route was blocked off by a wall enclosing the garden to the west and another row of parterre segments was added to fill in the space. The grandfather of the present owner, the Countess d'Entreves, built a greenhouse and a second house for lemon trees—or *limonaia*—on the terrace to accommodate the two hundred lemon trees that have always been a feature of this garden.

The garden plan is basically unchanged since its creation in the eighteenth century. There are two belvederes for views of the garden at either end of the villa. Within the villa walls is a pleasant shady courtyard with a very low box parterre and flowers that perfume the house.

Formerly on the north there was a wood with a *ragnaia*, or bird trap, and marble busts. The land slopes down to the north, the incline covered with olive trees. The city of Florence spreads across the valley in the distance.

The bright terrace garden is well maintained. There is a vast reservoir under the greenhouses. Three dogs romp in the garden together with baby tortoises.

Centuries ago, the villa was known as "La Torre," for an old tower on land of the Amidei family. This was sold in 1470 to Agnolo del Tovaglia, who built a magnificent villa with the architect Lorenzo da Monte Acuto. Although the exterior has been totally transformed, the grandeur of Tovaglia's villa is still evident in the interior. Tovaglia sold the property to the Florentine historian and politician Francesco Guicciardini. A plaque on the façade recalls that here Guicciardini wrote a portion of his *History of Italy*. This was probably around 1525, after the French were defeated at Pavia. From October 1529 until August 1530, Florence was under siege by imperialist forces at the

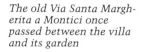

The old Via Santa Margherita a Montici once passed between the villa and its garden

A view from the garden belvedere

instigation of Pope Clement VII, whose Medici relatives had been ousted from power in Florence. Despite a gallant defense, the Florentines were greatly outnumbered. Furthermore, they had entrusted their forces within the city to a traitor, Malatesta Baglioni. Baglioni came to this villa in 1530 to meet with the enemy. He restrained his troops from pressing for victory in a successful sortie. More crucially, he did not send aid to the commander of the Florentine forces beyond the walls, who were decisively defeated at the Battle of Gavinana. Florence capitulated to the pope, losing its liberty as a republic with the return of the Medici. During the siege the villa was occupied by the commander of the enemy Italian mercenary soldiers, Sciarra Colonna. His troops left scars made by their pikes on the terracotta floor of the main salon that are still visible today. The name "La Bugia," meaning "falsehood" or "lie," might refer to the treachery of Baglioni.

In 1803 Francesco Morrocchi bought the villa from the Nerli family. Francesco's son Costantino completed the transformation of the villa in 1842. The garden is open by permission of the Countess d'Entreves.

Castello di Uzzano

Greve in Chianti
Gardens open to the public

The Castello di Uzzano has some of the prettiest gardens in Italy—
largely due to its setting amid the rolling Chianti hills. Vineyards and
olive groves are glimpsed through the umbrella pines around the castello. Flowers are abundant and more varied than in most Italian gardens.

The castle was built for the Uzzano family on a Roman-Etruscan
settlement sometime before the thirteenth century. The painter-
architect Andrea di Cione, called Orcagna, enlarged it in the
fourteenth century. The powerful Uzzano family made its fortune in
banking and provided Florence with several priors. The most illustrious owner of the property was the humanist Niccolo di Uzzano,
famed for his integrity and his animosity toward Cosimo de'Medici.
In 1478 the castle was fortified, anticipating an invasion of the Ara-
gonese. When hostilities ceased between Florence and Siena, the
Capponi family came into possession of the land, and the castle began its transformation from fortress to villa. The Capponi sold the
property in 1644 to Danielli Masetti da Bagnano. A century later, in
1754, Cavaliere Giulio Maria Baldassare Masetti modified the villa to
its present appearance. At this time the arcaded western façade with
double staircase and garden terraces were created. The Castello di
Uzzano again changed hands through marriage and is now the property of Count Briano Castelbarco Albani Masetti. A series of apartments for short-term rentals has been created in the forecourt.

Roses climb by the entrance gate of the castle's ivy-clad
forecourt. Red geraniums cascade over the green ivy from the windows of the rental apartments. A loggia leads to an inner courtyard of
the villa; here ivy trails down to the ground, moving slightly in the
breeze, ablaze with color in the autumn. A staircase with snapdragons growing up through cracks leads down to the upper terrace surrounding the villa. Here is a leaning fig tree, a horse chestnut, and
five types of cedars planted in the nineteenth century. In the south
corner, there is a flowerbed against a side staircase, and the *limonaia*.
A Baroque boxwood parterre in the shape of a wheel, with arabesques
between its spokes, dominates the southwest corner of the terrace.
Next to it a Baroque curved wall, topped with potted pink geraniums,

*A terracotta statue
stands in a dense maze of
clipped cypress*

Statuary in the sunken green garden

overlooks two flower gardens. Below is the cutting garden with beds of tulips, columbine, fox glove, zinnias, yarrow, and dahlias—according to the season. The garden here is gently shaded by a row of umbrella pines. Semi-circular steps lead up to a formal parterre with beds of alyssum, begonias, and lavender around a circle of pansies. This garden dates from the nineteenth century and is English in character. A hedge of clipped cypress closes this garden. We are on the level of the lower terrace and from here pass into a dense maze of shoulder high, clipped cypress with eighteenth-century terracotta statues of the Four Seasons, copied from those on the bridge of Santa Trinità in Florence. On the sides cypress is trained into arches. The labyrinths are trimmed in March and June. Beyond, steps lead down to a sunken formal garden with two reflecting pools. Towards the villa are sloping rectangular parterre beds filled with clipped box in geometrical designs. The steps are on an axis with the main façade of the villa, as well as to an approach allée of cypress. At the far northern end is a balcony overlooking a horseshoe-shaped green garden. Retracing steps, one arrives at the entrance of the woodland garden. A path meanders under pines and a sequoia, past rhododendrons, azaleas, and a charming thatched play house built in 1924. At the end is an allée of roses and then the villa.

The estate covers over twelve hundred acres, one hundred and fifty of which are vineyards. The remainder is a game preserve. The garden staff, under the able young head gardener Antonio, is augmented in the summer by ten foreign students who come to live at the castle.

The formal gardens have been reborn since 1984 under the guiding eye of Marion De Jacobert, manager of the estate of Castello di Uzzano. Walls have been rebuilt, beds replanted, and the pine forest successfully interspersed with rhododendrons and azaleas (normally azaleas are found in central Italy only in pots). She also oversees the efficient marketing of Castello di Uzzano wine and farm produce. Tomatoes from the gardens are sold in special sauces and served as *ribollita*, a Tuscan soup, at the small restaurant within the courtyard. The wines are of the finest quality, dating back from the time of Francesco Datini, the Merchant of Prato, whose cellar inventory in 1398 listed a wine from the Castello di Uzzano.

Mixed varieties of hanging ivy in the courtyard become a blaze of color in October

127 · *Castello di Uzzano*

Above:
After a mild winter, sur-
viving geraniums bloom
with renewed vigour,
cascading from the win-
dows of rental
apartments in the castle's
forecourt

Below:
Two small flower gardens
lie between a scalloped
wall and the cultivated
fields

Right:
Flowers and lemons grow
in profusion along the
terrace walls

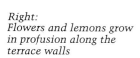

La Badia a Passignano

Passignano (near Florence-Siena Superstrada exit of Tavernelle)
Gardens open to the public

The hanging garden of the Badia a Passignano was planted in 1870, at a time when many gardens in Italy were being redesigned or newly laid out in the fashionable English landscape mode. That the garden of the Badia (or abbey) is in strict Classic Italian style follows the tendency among Florentines to perpetuate reactionary design canons. This was true especially among the old aristocracy, who saw the new landscape style as indicative of progressive, or foreign, ideas. The garden of the Badia a Passignano was made for the Polish count, Peduschi.

The Vallombrosan Abbey was founded by Saint Giovanni Gualberto in 1049. He was born in 985 at the nearby castle of Petrolo, and died at the abbey in 1073. His bones rest in the abbey church. In 1294 the monastery was rebuilt, with further amplifications in the fifteenth and sixteenth centuries. In the late sixteenth century the abbey became a center for scientific speculative studies under the direction of the abbot Ilario Alcei; Galileo served as one of the instructors. Napoleon, the self-appointed King of Italy, ordered the abbey to close in 1810. Count Peduschi obtained ownership of the abbey from the Italian state in 1870. It was returned to the Vallombrosan order on October 10, 1986.

To the right of the church is a door leading to the monastery. Its courtyard contains large magnolia trees and pots in which lemon trees, marigolds, and geraniums are all jumbled together in a blaze of color. A double-ramped staircase facing the entrance leads up to a large terrace with geraniums. The low surrounding walls are crenellated in Sienese Gothic style. The garden itself is meticulously kept up, the box carefully clipped into geometrical hedges. The central portion is composed of round topiary forms within square compartments. The rounded forms are repeated on the tops of the straight sides of the parterre borders. Some of the interior topiary is donut-shaped, planted with roses and lilies that relieve the predominantly green garden. A small putto holds a rod in a central octagonal marble pool. Pots of pink geraniums are placed on the corners of the fountain. Beyond the eastern wall is a curtain of tall dark cypresses. Opposite it, within the garden walls, is a long metal aviary beside a

A bed of herbs in the foreground supplies the monastery's kitchen and pharmacy. Beyond it are formal beds containing roses and lilies

greenhouse. A carefully tended vegetable garden is planted in front of these buildings. Busts of women are perched on the piers of the enclosing wall—a secular touch within the monastery.

Following:
A large central octagonal fish basin is graced by a putto

Villa di Fagnano

Fagnano
Gardens may be open to the
public upon request:
Pietro Terrosi
Vagnoli
Villa di Fagnano
Castelnuovo Berardenga
(Siena)

Near Vagliagli, three miles north of Siena, in the midst of the Chianti, an imposing *viale* (or avenue) of tall cypresses cuts across the plain, and turns, rising to the Villa di Fagnano. This extraordinary *viale*, over a mile in length, once had hedges of clipped yew dipping between each cypress. The villa, its *viale*, and grotto date back to the seventeenth century, designed by its owner, Giovan Battista Piccolomini in 1682.

The grotto is found midway up the viale, on the right. Facing a large rectangular fishpool, it consists of three large niches in the curving central block, and two flanking smaller ones set in straight lower walls. The central niche is equipped with water tricks, and has the Piccolomini arms on a marble shield above it. Statues are set in the side niches.

The grotto remains as it appears in eighteenth-century drawings at the Biblioteca Comunale of Siena, but the monumental staircase was unfortunately removed in the nineteenth century when the villa,

The nymphaeum *is set apart from the main garden*

as well, was transformed with crenellations into the Sienese Gothic style.

Apparently no garden ever existed in front of the villa. The slightly sunken formal garden is located at the southern side of the building. A gateway and enclosing fence are constructed from the barrels of arquebuses, acquired in 1777 when the Medici fortress in Siena was dismantled. The garden is composed of six square flowerbeds edged with low box hedges. Lemon pots are set at their corners. In the center is a small oval pool with a fine marble pedestal fountain, topped by a small statue of Neptune. Beyond the border of the pool are statues of the Four Seasons, copies of ones found in the royal gardens of Bulgaria. On an axis with the gate is the tiny green theater, raised up slightly beyond the fountain. Two cypress trees frame the stage and terracotta performing musicians flank it. To the right of the garden is a tall, domed aviary. A low wall separates the garden from a small ilex grove. In the mid-nineteenth century the park behind the villa was "updated" in the Romantic style, and winding paths were set between the pines and ilex.

The villa is part of a large agricultural estate, now owned by Pietro Terrosi Vagnoli. It has been in his family since 1920, when it was bought from the last descendents of the Piccolomini.

Villa di Catignano

Castelnuovo Berardenga
Gardens open upon request:
Signora Margherita Sergardi
Villa di Catignano
Castelnuovo Berardenga
(Siena)

Catignano's garden is full of activity due to a remarkable woman, Margherita Sergardi, who is a poet, playwright, director, and teacher. When the garden is not occupied by foreign visitors reading their paperback mysteries and soaking up the Tuscan sun, it becomes a stage for theatrical productions.

It is a recent garden, dating back to 1914 or 1915, but strongly inspired by traditional Italian models, and possibly following traces of a pre-existent seventeenth-century garden. Castelnuovo Berardenga on the outskirts of Siena was razed by the Spanish under Don Garzia of Toledo during the siege of 1554. Following this, Lodo-

Terracotta allegorical statues preside over theatrical performances held in the garden

The orchard and vege-
table garden of Catig-
nano

vico Sergardi commissioned Quinto Settano to build a villa on this site. (Lodovico Sergardi also built a second villa, nearer the city walls, Torre Fiorentina.) The garden as we know it was planned by Margherita Sergardi's mother.

A curving wall, topped by terracotta figures of animals and vases, closes off the large entrance courtyard of the villa. The wall is broken to the south by a double stairway which descends into the garden. The garden plan consists of four compartments of clipped box, symmetrically balanced, yet gently curving. Within are clipped, round shrubs—no flowers. The design focuses on a semicircle facing the stairway, referred to as "semicerchio d'Onestà" (or "Truth") by the owner. On tall pedestals are life-size female allegorical statues in terracotta. In the parterre are two large Atlas cedars (a species that only arrived in Europe in 1827). Against the wall of the staircase are beds with salvia, marigolds, and sunflowers. To the right, the garden is closed by a *limonaia* with an aviary. Beyond the parterre garden is an orchard, its trees interspersed with vegetables. Around the corner, bordering the orchard, is an enormous laurel, its branches forming a shady interior space. Behind the *limonaia* is a curious pattern of six long loops of clipped box, once filled with red geraniums. A greenhouse sits against the far end. Margherita Sergardi envisions this sec-

137 · *Villa di Catignano*

tion of the garden as the site of her next production, a play of Vittorio Alfieri. The hollowed out laurel bush will become a ticket office. The greenhouse will be filled with flames to represent hell, and heaven will be set on the terrace above.

In 1943, Margherita Sergardi taught the farmers of Catignano to perform traditional legends and dances. She became a professor of theater in Bologna for fifteen years, and formed the Piccolo Teatro di Siena. Her pupils now perform here in the gardens of Catignano. The first production was *La finestrina del cuore umano* (*The Little Window of the Human Heart*). In 1989 she produced a rewritten version of Molière's *Les Précieuses ridicules*. In honor of the anniversary of the French Revolution, the play celebrated the revolt of Arcadia, in which plants tied by the monarchy are liberated. The tradition of the green theater in Tuscan gardens is a strong one. Around Siena a number of these theaters survive, but they are rarely utilized.

Villa Torre Fiorentina

Siena
Gardens closed to the public

Just outside Siena's Porta Camollìa, on the Via Fiorentina, is the Villa Torre Fiorentina. Its terraced gardens have been much altered since the seventeenth century; they went through an English landscape phase in the eighteenth century, but in the early part of this century the formal division of flowerbeds was reinstated. (These have again been reorganized, simplifying the parterres.) The garden is included here because of its green theater, mercifully untampered with since its planting in the seventeenth century. The area around Siena is rich in garden theaters. This one can be compared to those of nearby Villa Gori, Villa Fagnano, and Villa Geggiano.

Plan from Triggs, The Art of Garden Design in Italy, *1906*

VILLA SERGARDI near SIENA *The Garden Theatre.*

Four high wings of clipped ilex stand behind the ilex proscenium on either side. The stage is slightly raked, rising to the rear. The proscenium is raised three feet above the level of the adjacent courtyard garden. A marble statue of Apollo stands in the center of the ilex backdrop. The stage is tiny; the courtyard, formed by the opposite building, now has large flowerbeds filled with bright red salvia and orange marigolds. Between the steep double staircase is a *nymphaeum* with a statue of Neptune.

The lower terrace is bordered by *limonaias;* a fish pool projects from the stone balustrade at the eastern end of the garden. In the far distance the peaceful Umbrian hills are visible. This section of the garden dates from 1920.

In 1799 the ailing Pope Pius VI rested here three days on his return to Rome from the Certosa of Florence. Another invalid, Richard Wagner, rented the villa for six weeks in 1880. He came here with his family, after a stay near Naples did not cure his erysipelas. Escaping the mid-August southern heat, Siena offered better air, the expense justified by his wife Cosima, "For people like us all extravagances have only one meaning, the achievement of peace and ease, so that the spirit can be free" (*Wagner,* Curt von Westernhagen, 1978). Apparently the visit achieved this; Wagner managed to finish the "drawing of bar lines," sketching out the orchestration for *Parsifal.* Liszt visited him here, describing the villa as "princely." Liszt played the music of *Parsifal* while Wagner sang it—perhaps performing on the little outdoor stage. Wagner was so impressed by the Cathedral of Siena that he later used it as his inspiration for the Temple of the Grail.

Villa Torre Fiorentina belongs to Baron Fabio Sergardi-Biringucci.

Belcaro

*Two miles west of Siena
Gardens open to the public
afternoons*

Plan from Triggs, The Art
of Garden Design in Italy,
1906

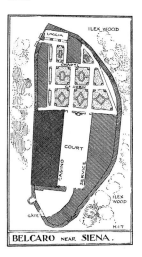

BELCARO NEAR SIENA.

*Following:
Within the walls of Bel-
caro, a simple garden
with lemon pots is set before the family chapel*

Belcaro as a garden is not a great beauty, but there are two important reasons to make a pilgrimage to this villa-fortress on the western outskirts of Siena. It retains its feel for the Medieval enclosed garden, or *hortus conclusus,* sheltered within crenellated castle walls, its garden visible from the ramparts. Secondly, it has great importance as an example of the Classical Italian integrated villa-garden design by one of the sixteenth-century's major architects, Baldassare Peruzzi of Siena. Its history goes back to the eleventh century. Belcaro belonged first to the Marescotti family, then to the Salimbeni as a fort, under whose ownership it was partially ruined in warfare. Saint Catherine of Siena later transformed it into a convent before it passed to the Augustinian order. Belcaro then became private property, held by various owners. Among them was the Turamini family, which hired Peruzzi between 1532 and 1535 to transform the fortress into a villa. His signed plan for the project is today in the Prints and Drawings department of the Uffizi in Florence. Peruzzi wisely retained the fortress walls, revamping the interior.

The castle is perched on top of a hill, surrounded by thick ilex woods. (Unfortunately, this has been allowed to grow unchecked over the years and now partially blocks the sweeping views from the ramparts.) One enters the first courtyard, angled and curved with a machicolated stone guard house. Passing through a wide archway, you arrive in a rectangular courtyard. On one side is a red brick façade; opposite is a typically Renaissance stone palace façade. Within the building are beautifully preserved frescoes by Peruzzi, with delicate grotesque decorations and scenes from mythology, including the Judgment of Paris. In the center is a well with two ancient buckets suspended above it. Two doors with wrought-iron gates lead into the garden beyond. Peruzzi's original plan called for the garden area to be walled off in three sections, the central and largest area reserved as a kitchen garden. To the left was intended a secret garden and a stairway to the ramparts. However, Peruzzi ultimately tucked a graceful Renaissance loggia and small chapel against the far wall. Both of these he frescoed, the loggia with trellised oranges and birds interspersed among lovely ornamental designs. The chapel frescoes have

A well with ancient buckets on the wall separates the garden from the inner courtard

Right:
The ramparts of the outer courtyards; the rebuilt villa is on the left

Below:
A fresco of the Judgment of Paris by Baldassare Peruzzi

been repainted. Where the secret garden was planned is now a long service building. The low hedges of box referred to in the beginning of the century have vanished, but lemon pots are still placed at the corners of the beds.

The villa reverted to its function of fortress in 1554, when it was bought by Gian Giacomo de' Medici. When the Florentines besieged Siena, the Medici captain Marignano used Belcaro as his headquarters. Belcaro is now privately owned, but open to the public.

Villa la Foce

Val d'Orcia
Gardens may be open upon
request:
Signora Benedetta Origo Crea
Villa la Foce
Chianciano Terme (Siena)

One of the most striking corners of Tuscany, Le Crete Senesi, or Sienese Clay, is found south of Siena. It is a desolate zone of lunar beauty, composed of worn clay hills, punctuated here and there by a line of cypresses, a clump of olives, and ageless farm houses which seem to be an outgrowth of the landscape itself. The newly married couple Marchese Antonio Origo and Iris Bayard Cutting chose to settle in the most barren part. They purchased over three thousand acres in 1924, cultivated the land, taught the local farmers new agricultural methods, and set up a small school and infirmary. They also sheltered soldiers from the advancing German forces in World War II. All of this is fascinatingly recounted by Iris Origo in her books *Images and Shadows* and *War in Val d'Orcia*.

Iris Origo came from a privileged, intellectual background. Her widowed mother, Lady Sybil Cuffe, moved to Florence from America in 1911, where she lived on the slopes of Fiesole in the historic Villa Medici. This had fifteenth-century gardens, restored by the English

The oldest part of the gardens

Right:
Stairs lead up to the rose garden and cypress walk

The latest section of the garden, designed by Cecil Pinsent

architect Cecil Pinsent in 1925. Pinsent worked in the Classical mode, in reaction to the English landscape garden style then prevalant. When the Origos were ready to plan their garden in Val d'Orcia, they turned to Pinsent. He designed a garden for them that was executed in stages subject to availability of water and funds. Using the natural sloping site, the garden is formed of terraces. The surrounding countryside becomes an element of the formal garden, which has belvederes and paths laid out along pretty views.

"La Foce," or The Outlet, refers to the joining of two valleys, the Val di Chiana and the Val d'Orcia. The buildings were an old inn and grain warehouse, formerly owned by the sisters of the Scale Mieli Salva Dio around 1800. The Origos added a wing for their living quarters and renovated the farm buildings. The formal gardens stretch to the rear of the villa. The first necessity was water, met by the wedding gift of Iris Origo's American grandmother who gave them a pipe line stretching six miles from a hilltop spring. The water now gushes with abundant force, keeping the garden verdant through scorching summers.

The first section Pinsent designed for them, in 1934, was adjacent to the house, a small formal Italian enclosed garden with box hedges, flowerbeds, and a dolphin fountain set in a low stone basin in the middle of the lawn. A pergola borders the villa wall against the wing, and a loggia overlooks the garden. Above it, against the hillside, is a laurel hedge. Just below it is a small lemon court with high hedges. A door from the house leads into it, and a ramp leads up to the formal fountain garden.

The second zone of the garden is a large, terraced area made in 1936. The ripples of the hillside are incorporated into formal divisions of clipped box which surround grassy squares set with lemon pots and banksia roses. A wall overlooking the valley is topped with carved stone urns. Beneath it is a bed of dahlias. At the far end of the terrace is a balcony overlooking a garden, which "on summer nights," wrote Iris Origo, "would be alight with fireflies and the air heavy with nicotiana and jasmine" (*Images and Shadows*, Origo, 1970). The walls of this garden are covered in spring with alyssum and aubrietia, followed by climbing roses. A bisecting path leads through the garden up the hillside and traverses the rose garden. It then continues up through the woods, a cypress allée marking the route which leads to a chapel. The Origos only son Gianni was buried here in 1933. The woods are filled with daffodils, scillas, crocus, cyclamen, and wild violets. Returning to the rose garden, the path twists around the contour of the hillside.

The third and final section of the garden is reached from the large terrace. In 1956 Cecil Pinsent designed this formal, sunken, green garden on a wedge-shaped plot. The site is gently sloped upwards the narrow end. The box divisions are clipped in tiers, designed in perspective to make the garden appear longer than it is in fact.

Four large magnolia trees are planted facing the retaining stair wall, which has a grotto in its center. At the far end, a low pool is set in the lawn before a stone monument of Hercules.

To wander further up the hillside brings you to a semi-wild garden with scented long rows of lavender, masses of thyme, and mint.

Iris Origo experimented with her garden, learning what would adapt to the drying hot winds and frigid winters. She said she gave up on delphiniums, phlox, lupins, and many other herbaceous plants. It was possible to have lemons, plumbago, and jasmine only if properly protected in the winter. She discovered that lilies and roses thrived in the heavy clay soil and lavender took to the hillside, "a blue sea in June, buzzing with the bees whose honey is flavored with its pungent taste, which also, in the winter, not only scents our linen but kindles our fires"(*Images and Shadows*).

In front of the villa, to the side of the entrance drive, is a sunny lawn. Here is the *limonaia* (lemon greenhouse), used in the summer as a pool house. Nearby, a modern sculpture of a horseman and bulls is set in a small fountain. A side entrance is approached through a small, formal green garden with high hedges and clipped box.

Iris Origo is best remembered for her biographies of Lord Byron, Giacomo Leopardi, San Bernardino, and Francesco Datini, the Merchant of Prato. She died in 1988, leaving La Foce to her daughter. A cultural society, Incontri in Terra di Siena, was founded in 1989 in memory of Iris and Antonio Origo. It sponsors summer concerts at La Foce.

Staircase leading down to the garden of Hercules

Villa Farina

Val d'Esse di Cortona
Gardens may be open upon
request:
Villa la Farina
Il Campaccio
Val d'Esse di Cortona

A garden in decay can have a poignant charm. This one proudly retains the lines of its layout, yet the vegetation that gave definition to the garden is in places hopelessly overgrown. *Campaccio* means a worthless field, implying hardship for its caretaker. This is the name given to the grounds of what is now known as Villa Farina.

At Il Campaccio there are no flowers to speak of, no beautiful statuary or fountains. And yet, there are places that fascinate for their breadth of conception—and this is one of them. The network of allées takes possession of a strongly sloping hillside; ilex becomes a building material to construct a theater and a basilica. This was not the site of a lavish court or the suburban home of a powerful noble, near a major city. We are on the outskirts of Cortona, a small historic city in eastern Tuscany.

Originally there was just a farm house, owned by the Orselli family. In 1751 this was inherited by Galeotto Corazzi-Ridolfini—a cultivated man who was passionate about archaeology and a collector of Roman and Etruscan artifacts, with his own museum in Cortona. (Eventually these pieces found their way to a museum in Leiden, Holland.) He and many others of his family were members of the Accademia Etrusca. Their meetings, Le Notti Cortiane, were held in members' houses, although there are no written records of such rendezvous at Villa Farina. Galeotto was also a Cavaliere di Malta, a member of an ancient Catholic charitable order.

There are no documents to establish that the basic structure of the garden was planned by Galeotto, but no doubt he or his son Francesco had a major hand in it. Francesco died childless in 1788; soon afterwards, the estate passed through the hands of his three nephews. There appeared the first record of the garden in the 1803 *catasto* (a property description for taxation purposes). It describes a greenhouse, fountains, gates, pyramids, a grotto, perspective garden, and aqueducts, all surrounded by a wall. The garden appears again in the 1826 *catasto*, which describes the territory of Cortona for the Lorraine regime. The original portion of the garden predates the mode for "English landscape," which reached Italy about 1780. Thus the earlier half of the garden could conceivably date from 1700 to 1760. France-

The fields of Il Campaccio, planted with vines and traversed by a cypress allée

sco's grand nephew Giuseppe took possession in 1856. It is due to Giuseppe Ridolfini that the garden took its present form. He added to the east a landscape garden with hunting pavilion, ornamental lake, and a green theater, and probably also altered the apses of the basilica and built the spring house. Giuseppe's heir, his granddaughter Annunziata Minozzi, held the property briefly in 1895. It then passed to Alberto Fraschetto, who altered the entrance approach to the villa and drained the stagnant lake. Around 1925, Emilio Farina bought the property. Since 1911, no changes have been made to the garden. The entrance winds past an elliptical pool, up to the villa. The villa is not on a true axis with the garden; in an attempt to align it, a pincer-shaped staircase was added to a corner of the house. From here the eye is led across the central allée of ilex to the hunting pavilion at the east end of the property. This allée is bisected at a right angle by a double row of cypresses which leads up the slope to the north boundary wall. The cypress allée is an impressive sight, cutting through the fields. In the mid-nineteenth century, Giuseppe Ridolfini planted an interior row of cypresses, alternating with the older outer ones. By pruning, these new cypresses were kept on a dwarf scale, enhancing the perspective, which terminated in a frescoed scene on the garden wall. This fresco, depicting a temple, is much faded today, but a side scene still shows an Etruscan tripod which was an emblem of the Accademia Etrusca. A Doric column stands before the wall. The small hunting pavilion in Neoclassical style resembles a small temple. In front of it is an open oval area, the eastern termination point of the main ilex avenue. This was spread with nets to trap birds. Here Giuseppe created a romantic park in the current mode, with meandering paths of viburnum, leading through a wood to a small lake with a grotto and island, patterned on the lake at the Villa Reale at Monza.

According to the local newspaper, at that time the countryside was suffering hardships agriculturally, alleviated by the employment Ridolfini gave to create his garden. There are two further allées—one of tunnel-shaped ilex. In between these allées are fields planted with vineyards and olives. The farm is totally integrated with the formal garden elements. Of great interest is the so-called basilica. Originally it had three apses; now the one bordering the northern wall has been transformed with a steep staircase that leads to a belvedere platform. Three aisles of the nave are defined by low stone walls and rows of ilex. Once clipped to form walls, the ilex trunks appeared as columns, but today they have regrettably grown beyond recuperation. The northern wall has been altered to include a gate into the adjacent farm fields. There one finds a rectangular, Renaissance-style reservoir tank and the traces of a *ragnaia,* or bird-hunting trap, constructed of ilex. Back near the entrance of the basilica is a rusticated stone building of one room, which serves as a spring house or grotto. There is a curious tunnel that approaches this, built in the guise of an Etruscan tomb.

The main east-west axis is planted with ilex, which, until about twenty years ago, were clipped in spherical shapes.

Ridolfini's most intriguing addition was the green theater, in concept a throwback to Classical Italian garden design. Built against the hillside, double rows of ilex were planted in horseshoe formation. The interior row was clipped as an arcade, creating "boxes" for the audience. In August 1963 the theater was revived; Corrado Pavolini directed a production of *I Cinque Disperati,* which attracted too large an audience for the little theater. The actual performance had to be shifted to the drained lake to accommodate the crowds. With replanting it is possible that the theater could be restored; at this writing, however, it is sadly overgrown. This garden has been the subject of an intensive study by architectural students Maria Cristina Mazzecchi and Roberto Severi in the University of Florence garden restoration program, under Francesco Gurrieri. Although this garden is not yet under state protection, it is hoped that the attention focused on it will lead to its conservation.

Three Gardens of Cortona

The garden of Villa Venuti di Catrosse, Cortona, is open to the public

For permission to visit others write:

Villa Passerini Pergo (Cortona)

Villa Sandrelli Alberto Sandrelli Camucia (Cortona)

In addition to the garden of Il Campaccio or Villa Farina, there are three other gardens worthy of interest on the outskirts of Cortona.

La Villa Venuti di Catrosse is found about a mile out of the gate of Santa Maria of Cortona. Pre-existing buildings belonging to the Venuti family since the fifteenth century were incorporated into a new construction between 1725 and 1729, following the design of the Florentine architect Alessandro Galilei. He also envisioned a walled garden and extended park, with a *bosco* of ilex and hedges of box, cypress, and laurel. His hydraulic expertise was put into play bringing water to the fountains from neighboring springs. The owner, Domenico Girolamo Venuti, tax auditor to the Tuscan Grand Duke, died

Villa Catrosse, project of M. Tuscher, from the collection of M. Gori Sassoli

The frescoed limonaia *of Villa Passerini*

in 1729, leaving the unfinished property to his brother's five sons. In 1730 the ownership was assumed totally by the eldest of the nephews, Marcello. He spent much of his time in Naples and was instrumental in the discovery of Herculaneum. Marcello Venuti had a German architect, Marcus Tuscher, prepare a revised plan for the villa. This project was engraved in 1738, showing garden rooms on a terraced site. The walled lemon garden still exists today, albeit in a pitiful state. The gates, the round central pool, and the steps descending to the lower portion of the walled garden are all still in place. The plaster-covered walls have ornamental volutes, and an opening is now enlarged into a side entrance gate. Rusticated gates opened onto the adjacent gardens. The pavilion at the far end of the walled garden was never realized, nor was the formal, sweeping double staircase in front of the villa. Tuscher's plan called for tall hedges around a fountain on the top level and a boat basin below. A *bosco* was planted in front of the oratory. At Marcello's death in 1755 the villa was inherited by his eldest son, Giuseppe Benvenuto Venuti, who did not resume work on it until 1774. At that time an architect of Cortona, Onofrio Boni, drew up designs in the Neoclassical style for a casino and coffeehouse, but the buildings were never realized.

A second garden outside Cortona at Camucia, Villa Sandrelli, has vestiges of its late eighteenth-century origins. Dating from 1768, it was originally a large farm house belonging to the Tommasi family. It passed by marriage in the early nineteenth century to the Sergardi; in 1930 it was purchased by the Sandrelli family, who still own it. The rectangular garden is to the rear of the villa and connecting farm buildings. At either end are gates opening onto semicircular areas beyond the enclosed garden. The area directly behind the villa was altered in the late nineteenth century: a large magnolia took the place of a fountain and pines were added for shade. A low wall sets off the former adjacent orchard. The mother of the current owner, Alberto Sandrelli, designed the parterre around a basin. Low clipped hedges and a grapevine pergola occupy this area. The right wall dips down to allow a view of the surrounding countryside. Formerly, the enclosing walls had statues of *pietra serena* and twenty lemon plants stood beyond the gate in the semicircle. The garden slopes down at the far end. Remains of a *bosco* and a vegetable garden frame eighteenth-century niches. One facing the villa contains a statue of a man pouring water. This niche is part of a clock tower, which once had a bell on top of it. The counterpart of this niche is facing the farm house, and contains the figure of a woman. The backgrounds are painted in vivid colors, traditionally representing day and night. The enclosed gardens set off the villa from the working farm, providing privacy and protection.

Villa Passerini at Pergo is another farm house which has gradually been enlarged since the sixteenth century to become a comfortable villa. Originally owned by the Mancini family, it passed by inheritance around 1850 to the Passerini family of Florence. The approach road passes a large walled fishpond, or reservoir, with a stone bridge linking a grassy island to the shore. A splendid ancient plane tree dominates the drive. The land slopes gently down and is terraced with low walls for cultivation. To the left of the villa is a small formal garden with flowerbeds around a central basin. Orange trees grow by the gates. A tiny loggia is tucked in a corner, and a small fountain flows beside a wall. Facing the main gate is the orange house with a decorative portal surmounted by a clock. The interior of the orange house is luminous, its walls having been frescoed in the nineteenth century with red swags and geometrical decorations. Napoleonic soldiers are painted on its walls, recalling the French occupation of Italy. The effect is playful and unusual. To the right of the garden is a small door leading to a courtyard facing the family chapel. This was formerly planted in parterre design; the stone border edgings still exist. Now, within this sheltered spot, there are an old magnolia and ancient camellias that bloom in February.

Villa Fedelia

Spello
Gardens open to the public
on Thursdays, Saturdays,
Sundays

Umbria is not noted for its formal gardens. Perhaps the lack of them is due to economic factors. After the Renaissance, the area did not attract great wealth. Much of Umbria is hilly, difficult farming terrain. The gardens that exist are apt to be small. Two diminutive historic gardens stand out: the hanging garden of the Ducal Palace in Urbino, and the cloister of San Damiano at Assisi. A surviving exception to the rule is the garden of Villa Fedelia, outside Spello. This, however, was originally laid out by a Roman who settled here.

The site of Villa Fedelia has a fascinating history. During the fourth century permission was given to the people of Hispellum (or Spello) by the emperor to hold annual games in the town on the condition that they build a large and magnificent temple to the Gens Flavia, as the area around Spello was known. This temple stood on the hillside now occupied by the villa and its gardens. During the Middle Ages the temple compound was torn apart for its stone. Adjacent to the property is the oratory of San Fedele, in memory of a martyred local bishop. Hence the name of Villa Fedelia.

The family of Acuti Urbani were noted in Spello from 1210 when they were made Cavalieri and Counts Palatine by Holy Roman Emperor Otto IV. From an early date they owned this property, finally building a suburban villa here at the end of the fifteenth century on the foundations of a chapel dedicated to Venus. The Urbani family died out early in the eighteenth century.

Villa Fedelia was then bought by Teresa Pamphili Grillo. She had fled Rome, where she had been unhappily married, and in her travels stopped in Spello, where she decided to rebuild her life. She was noted for her charitable works and her piety. In the early years of the eighteenth century, she laid out the garden on an axis with the villa on the highest terrace of the old Roman temple ruins. The garden's relationship to the villa recalls Villa Medici in Fiesole and Villa Madama in Rome. Against the hillside a retaining wall is enlivened with niches. The long rectangular garden is subdivided into two rows of waist-high box hedges enclosing herbs. Lemon pots and stone vases decorate the garden. A small wisteria-covered belvedere looks out onto the vast plain to the west. Behind this sunny shelf, the hill rises

up with a shady *bosco* with paths and cypress-lined carriage drives.

After the death of Teresa Pamphili Grillo, the villa passed to Count Sperelli, and then to a rich landowner, Gregorio Piermarini. By 1830 Piermarini had built a new small villa, the so-called Casino di Villeggiatura. A drawing of this date by engineer Saverio Andreucci shows the casino and surrounding gardens, vineyards, and orchards. A new garden to the northwest of the casino was planted on the slope extending down to the main road to Perugia. This is a rising perspective garden of green lawns, bordered by dark cypresses and holm oak. The progression is broken halfway by a wall surmounted by a statue of Diana the Huntress and the entrance drive to the casino. Clipped boxwoods pattern the area behind Diana, and curving flights of steps form an amphitheater. The perspective culminates in a multi-storied, niched exedra, tinted in bright pumpkin and raspberry. It is thought that both the casino and the perspective garden are the work of a relative, the noted architect Giuseppe Piermarini.

Gregorio Piermarini died in 1845. The villa then passed through the Tani-Menicacci family to the Collegio Vitale Rosi. The last private owners were the Costanzi family, who made modifications to the designs of Cesare Bazzani after 1925. They sold the old villa to the sisters of the Missionarie d'Egitto to be used as a convent. The casino and gardens were sold to the province of Perugia. In 1930 the king of Bulgaria, Boris, and his bride, Queen Giovanna, spent part of their honeymoon here.

Cypresses accent the sloping garden

Villa Caprile

Pesaro
Gardens open to the public;
tours given in July and August

Gardens on the Adriatic coast are typically walled to protect delicate plants from harsh winds off the sea. Villa Caprile's tiered garden is enclosed at two levels: the courtyard behind the villa, and the principal middle terrace on the southern slope beneath it.

Despite war damage and minimal alterations, the garden has been restored and fortunately maintained, thanks to the presence of an agricultural college. The school's curriculum includes work in the gardens. One could only wish that more Italian gardens in threatened condition were turned over to agricultural institutions.

Villa Caprile was once considered an obligatory stop for any visitor of note to Pesaro. In 1772 Giovanni Giacomo Casanova stayed here for five days, guest of Marquis Carlo Mosca Barzi. Stendhal mentions his visit in his diary. Ferdinand IV, duke of Parma, came in 1795 as guest of Marquis Francesco Mosca. The composer Gioacchino Antonio Rossini lived here, as did Princess Caroline of Brunswick.

The Toschi-Mosca were of Bergamasque origin, transferring to Pesaro in 1550 when invested with the Rocca of Gradara. The property was known as "Caprile." Originally it had a hunting lodge, which was rebuilt as a summer villa in 1640 by Giovanni Mosca. Over the years the villa and gardens were added to, especially in 1763 under Marquis Carlo Mosca Barzi. His son Francesco continued the work. The garden as it exists today dates from this period. In 1887 the property became an agricultural school.

The original main approach led down to the Via Flaminia. It ends at the lowest terrace, the basin of Atlas. This entrance proved too steep to be practical, so the entrance today is from the side. In the past this side road was lined with elms. There were two large wooden gates which have vanished and a pavement mosaic with the coat of arms of the Mosca family that concealed water jets—also now gone. The garden of Villa Caprile is remarkable for its ingenious water system; many of its water tricks are still operable today. Under the box hedges are one thousand little holes for irrigation. Water is brought to the garden through the hills a mile away to gather in underground reservoirs.

The balustraded terrace in front of the villa serves as a belvedere

A corner of the main terrace with formal box-enclosed flowerbeds

overlooking the gardens below and the city in the distance. A double-ramped staircase containing the grottoes descends to the main garden terrace. Wisteria grows against the walls and lemon trees are planted in the ground—rare in an Italian garden, as lemon trees are usually potted. Through a rose-covered gate one passes beyond the walled garden to the fields beyond. Facing the gate is an allée of carefully clipped, cone-shaped yews leading to the green theater of cypress trees.

On one side of the allée are greenhouses, on the other fruit trees. Returning to the center terrace, the grottoes offer cool shelter. There are three grottoes decorated with pebbles and shells. One contains a wooden devil with water flowing from his mouth, trident, and horns; his eyes and tongue move. In the past, on the opposite side of this grotto was the cavern of the Cyclops, with bronze figures hammering on an anvil. In the central grotto is a revolving scene of Neptune. Water pressure causes Neptune to shake his head and trident; the god is followed by sirens and creatures of the sea. Birds sing on branches and a star spins until water pours down on the visitor from the ceiling, together with drenching jets from the pavement and walls. At the entrance of this grotto are basins with dolphins. The grotto to the far left had a water clock with moving spheres, marking the hours with water jets. Outside on the stairwall is a niche containing a statue hiding the "cuckoo." When the cuckoo's song ends, a jet sprays the visitor. Also within this terrace is a stone disc surrounded by jets producing a rainbow effect in the sunlight.

The third level is narrower. Four rectangular beds surround an old basin. The lemon trees here have been placed in pots.

The fourth and lowest level has been somewhat crudely rebuilt. Flanked by two curving flights of steps, the basin of Atlas contains various bits and pieces of sculpture and architectural details.

Villa Caprile was badly damaged in an earthquake in 1916 and by gunfire in 1940. The green theater has been replanted, and sandstone architectural elements have been copied in cement and tinted.

The central fountain overgrown with moss and flowers

Villa Imperiale

Pesaro
Gardens open to the public via
summer tours:
Azienda di Soggiorno
Via Rossini 41
Pesaro

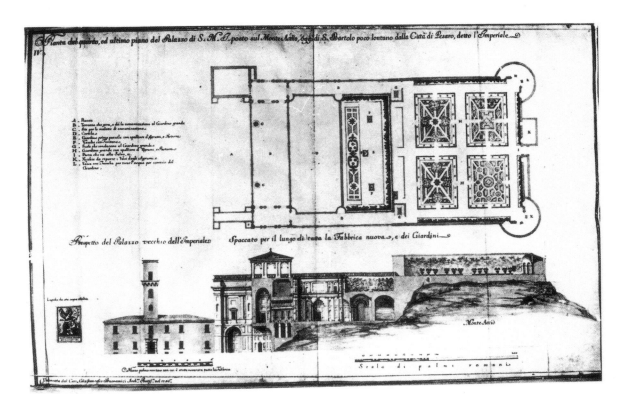

Plan from Boriosi, I Giardini d'Italia, *1970*

The gardens of the Villa Imperiale at Pesaro are a direct outgrowth of
Rome's Villa Madama and the Vatican's Belvedere. Raphael's letter
describing his designs for Villa Madama to Baldassare Castiglione was
used by the architect Girolamo Genga of Urbino for its concept of
interpenetrating porticoed courtyard and tightly linked, multileveled
terraces. As at Villa Madama, surrounding views were important.
Here the San Bartolo hills are seen from roof corridors joined to the
garden terraces. The ascending triple garden levels, excavated against
the hillside, reflect the design of the Vatican Belvedere.

The name "Imperiale" commemorates the visit of the Holy Roman Emperor Frederick III, who placed the first stone in 1452. En route from his coronation in Rome, he was a guest here of Alessandro Sforza, then governor of Pesaro. Genga studied painting in Rome during the construction of the pleasure pavilion Villa Farnesina and thus Villa Imperiale was also known as the "Farnesina of Pesaro."

Entrance to the villa's courtyards

The main courtyard garden

A formal broderie *garden with a pebble background, beyond the walls of the villa*

The original Palazzo Imperiale, finished in 1472, remains at the base of the hill—its tower is intact, minus the old crenellations. Joined to it between 1522 and 1531 is Genga's creation, built for Eleanora Gonzaga, wife of Francesco Maria I della Rovere. It became Francesco's favorite residence. The new structure reached from the old building up the hillside. Its most striking feature is its beautifully proportioned, U-shaped courtyard with niches and a deep vaulted portico for theatrical performances, strongly reminiscent of Villa Madama. Off the courtyard are rocaille-encrusted chambers with fountains for cool dining. The Greek bronze statue of the "Idolino of Pesaro" once stood in the center of the courtyard; now it is a prize exhibit of the Archaeological Museum in Florence. The square and rectangular flowerbeds filled with begonias date from the nineteenth century.

Concealed within the walls of the courtyard are intricate spiral stairs leading up to the big terrace and the secret hanging garden on a level with the state rooms. Genga designed an extensive terrace walk with loggias around the courtyard, linking it to the top-level garden by an archway. The narrow secret garden has low geometric borders framing the flowerbeds. A row of lemon trees grows against the retaining wall of the large garden above, which serves as a sheltering sup-

port for a winter greenhouse. Duchess Eleanora corresponded with her administrator about the planting of this level, which then had espaliered bitter oranges against the wall, thirty-four citrons, two lemons, and hybrids brought from Savona.

Side stairs bring the visitor to the highest level—a vast parterre garden with four beds. In Eleanora's day the paths were covered with grape arbors bordered by hedges of laurel and roses. In the parterres were three sailboats of laurel and myrtle. The enclosing walls formed an outdoor room, sheltering the garden from harsh winds. In the corners were semicircular loggias. Formerly, one could pass through a gate in this garden into the pine forest, and then follow a path to the nearby Villa della Vedetta on the crest of the hill. (Villa della Vedetta, built in 1583, was unique among Renaissance villas as it was built on the edge of the sea.)

Outside the palace walls is a sunken, formal garden. The low box is clipped in an elaborate pattern, its green box contrasting with a white pebble background.

Typically Renaissance, the gardens of Villa Imperiale are enclosed and on an axial plan with a wood beyond the formal gardens. Here in the Marche, gardens remained conservative in their design and tended to be sheltered, sunny havens from the Adriatic winds until the eighteenth-century landscape mode took hold. This garden was famed for its unusual variety of fruits and trees.

Giorgio Vasari praised Genga's work in *The Lives of the Italian Painters, Sculptors, and Architects:* "It is a beautiful structure, full of chambers, colonnades and courts, loggias and fountains, and pleasant gardens, so that all princes passing that way go to see it, and among them Paul II when he went to Bologna with his court, who was greatly delighted" and no doubt came away with ideas for his own Orti Farnesiani in Rome. The poet Bernardo Tasso speaks of the villa in the second volume of his *Letters.* In his epic *Rinaldo* Torquato Tasso based his Palazzo della Cortesia on Villa Imperiale.

The last of the della Rovere—Vittoria—married Ferdinando II de' Medici and moved to Florence in 1634. The villa's decline dates from her departure. Thanks to the unstinting efforts of Count Clemente Castelbarco-Albani, the garden has been reborn since the end of World War II.

III *Latium*
Campania

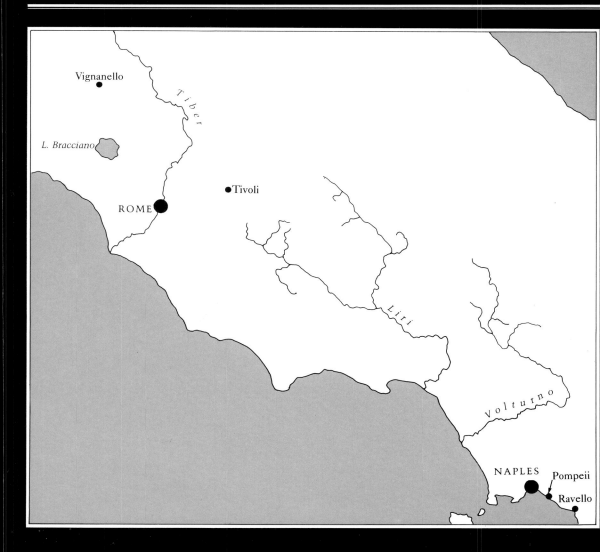

Vignanello

Tiber

L. Bracciano

ROME

Tivoli

Liri

Volturno

NAPLES Pompeii

Ravello

Castello Ruspoli

Vignanello
Gardens open upon request:
Prince Alessandro Ruspoli
Castello Ruspoli
Vignanello (Viterbo)

Right:
The lower garden, its wall covered with straw-berry grapes and roses

Below:
A section of the initialed parterre, dating from 1530–1531

Vignanello is a time capsule of a feudal village. At one end of the main street is a moated, twelfth-century fortress castle, its formal garden and hunting park behind it reached by a bridge. The garden contains the most important original box parterre surviving in Italy, dating from the early seventeenth century.

Pope Paul III presented a castle to a relative, Ortensia Farnese, in 1536. It descended through her husband's family, the Marescotti, until 1709, when Francesco Marescotti married Vittoria Ruspoli—the last of her line—and assumed her surname. The Ruspoli were made

papal princes for their services to Pope Innocent XIII early in the eighteenth century. They were also related to the pope by marriage. Within the castle, now used as a summer residence, are mementos of the future pope's visit in 1720, relics of Saint Giacinta, born Clarice Marescotti, and photographs of the grandfather of the present owner, Alessandro Ruspoli, a bonvivant, huntsman, and last grand master of the Vatican.

The garden was first laid out between 1530 and 1531. Its box parterre was originally formed of rosemary. The parterre, planted in the shape of initials, is sited directly under the windows of the castle, just beyond the moat, and is intended to be viewed from above. It consists of twelve square compartments: the central ones spell out the initials OO, enclosing a G and an S. Ottavia Orsini, daughter of Vicino Orsini (whose fantastic garden of Bomarzo is nearby), married Marc'Antonio Marescotti in 1574. Widowed sometime between 1600 and 1612, Ottavia was guardian of her sons Sforza and Galeazzo. By 1618 Sforza attained his majority. Since Marc'Antonio's initials do not appear here, this parterre must have been planted between 1600 and 1618. The castle remains as it was in Ottavia's time.

Fifty potted lemon trees are distributed around the parterre garden. A lower garden is set to the right below it. A long curving wedge against the parterre wall, it has a series of circular box flowerbeds, and dates from the beginning of the twentieth century. Strawberry grapes and roses climb its walls. Beyond the parterre garden is a vast hunting park. At its entrance is a column with the Ruspoli coat of arms. This was the Column of Justice which stood in the town piazza until fifty years ago. Transgressors who used bad language were manacled here to the column in public. Today the townspeople are requesting the return of this monument to feudal power, to be incorporated into a fountain. Castello Ruspoli is now owned by Prince Alessandro Ruspoli.

Villa Giulia

Rome
*Gardens of Museo Nazionale
Etrusco open to the public*

Villa Giulia is the last of the great Roman suburban Renaissance villas. Located above Piazza del Popolo on the Viale delle Belle Arti, its property is much reduced from the sixteenth century.

Originally, the land belonged to Cardinal Antonio Fabiani del Monte. He left it to his nephew, Ciocchi del Monte, who became Pope Julius III in 1550. As pope, Julius transformed the property into a lavish papal retreat. A long steep allée linked the villa to the banks of the Tiber and the papal barge landing.

What remains of the garden is integrated with the villa, a series of true "garden rooms"—or extensions of the villa—here confined not with hedges, but with masonry walls, linked together with great sophistication. The series of courtyards is designed according to Renaissance canon on the main axis of the casino and is designed to pro-

Plan from Triggs, The Art of Garden Design in Italy, *1906*

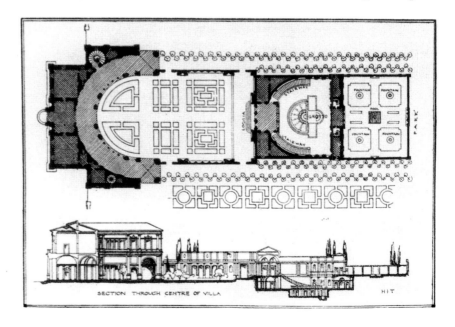

vide a chain of perspective viewpoints. A large horseshoe-shaped courtyard leads up to a second smaller courtyard with multiple levels. On either side of the courtyards on the main axis are long, narrow gardens, which originally were probably kitchen and secret gardens.

Actual construction began in May 1552. Vasari in *The Lives of the Italian Painters, Sculptors, and Architects* gives himself credit for the main design, especially for the *nymphaeum*, but today it is believed that Bartolommeo Ammannati had a greater hand in its design. Jacopo Barozzi Vignola worked on the construction until 1555. Michelangelo was also consulted on the design, and the pope himself added his thoughts.

The main courtyard's peristyle vault was frescoed by Taddeo Zuccaro with a trellis design and links the casino interior to the garden beyond. The walls of the garden are broken up with niches which once contained the considerable collection of antiquities assembled by Pope Julius III. His successor, Paul IV, hauled off the art works to the Vatican, where they remain today. In the second courtyard a large semicircular balustrade encloses the remarkable grotto below it. This celebrates the Acqua Vergine, one of the water supplies of Rome, a concept borrowed from Classical times, when special fountain shrines, or *nymphaeum*, were built to mark sources of water. The floor is patterned with an antique mosaic depicting a sea satyr with squid. On the terrace level twin staircases sweep up to a Serlian loggia. The long, narrow side gardens contain a reconstructed Etruscan temple and box-enclosed flowerbeds under towering maritime pines.

Since 1889 Villa Giulia has been a museum of antiquities, now known as the Museo Nazionale.

Villa of the Knights of Malta

Rome
Gardens open to the public
Wednesday to Friday morn-
ings upon request:
Ordine dei Cavalieri di Malta
Via Condotti 68
Rome

*Roses in the garden of
the Knights of Malta*

High on the Aventine hill there is a patch of calm in chaotic Rome. This is basically a residential zone, but also a diplomatic corner, so police cars stand by in the bizarre little piazza. Around its walls are broad stone benches and large bas-reliefs of military trophies. Obelisks and urns top the walls. The main source of activity during the daylight hours appears to be private limousines that discharge tourists who peer through the famous keyhole into the garden of the Villa of the Knights of Malta. They see a long, dark green allée framing the vista of the dome of Saint Peter's nearly two miles across the Tiber River.

The Knights of Malta, or Ordine dei Cavalieri di Malta, originally were known as the Knights of Saint John of Jerusalem. They began as hospitallers in Jerusalem before the First Crusade, providing shelter for pilgrims. The order took on a military character with the onset of the Crusades. Driven from Jerusalem in 1187, they settled in Acre. In the thirteenth century the Moslems expelled them, and Cyprus became their headquarters, whereupon they entered into a grand naval career. After capturing Rhodes in 1310, the order moved there. They absorbed much of the wealth of their rival order, the suppressed Knights Templars, and became extremely powerful. Branches were established in other countries, including Italy—home of the original founders who were from Amalfi. In 1522, after a six-month siege, Suleiman I conquered Rhodes and the Knights were forced to leave. The emperor Charles V granted them the Island of Malta for their headquarters, and they became known as the Knights of Malta. The French in 1798 evicted the order from Malta and confiscated their considerable portable wealth. A two-year siege followed, and the Maltese held out against recapture by the French until the British came to their assistance. Headquarters of the order were shifted to Rome in 1834, where they remain today. The Order of Saint John was revived with the Treaty of Amiens, but was subjected to certain limitations.

Rome operates as headquarters for the order's charitable operations. Here the Knights enjoy extraterritorial diplomatic privileges. Their villa is perched on the edge of a precipice, site of a former fortress. The compound consists of two large buildings, a medieval chapel renovated by Giambattista Piranesi, plus the garden. It is believed that Piranesi put his hand to the design of the garden itself, with its coffeehouse and priory tower. The bird's-eye-view map of Rome by Giambattista Nolli, done in 1718 before Piranesi began work, shows two preexisting parterres with simply patterned flowerbeds and the allée with two rows of plantings.

The entrance courtyard has touches of domesticity, laundry stretched out to dry in the hot sun beside a marble well brimming over with pink geraniums. Against an inner wall is a fountain with aquatic plants. From here one passes into a large parterre area full of bright pansies and pink petunias set in diamond-shaped compartments, or box-edged, Maltese cross pattern. This section of the garden is slightly sunken, designed to be viewed from the windows of the opposite priory. At the far end by the chapel walls are greenhouses. The walls of the villa are covered with jasmine. Toward the piazza adjacent to the sunny parterre section, is a second garden, a shady haven. Here a cedar of Lebanon and big magnolias shelter a goldfish pool. Calla lilies, ferns, and hydrangea are set in pots along paths. Tiny pheasant chicks scurry under low-lying foliage, and an aged, lumbering shepherd dog makes his rounds about the garden. The surrounding walls have wonderfully decorated niches, peopled with busts

In the parterre a Maltese cross is depicted in box-wood

of worthies.

A series of three allées runs from the piazza wall to the balus-traded edge. These cool, dark, vaulted walkways are planted with box and laurel. Within them, overlooking the formal parterre, is the buff-colored coffeehouse, a simple stucco pavilion with two arched openings. Inside are the coats of arms of past grand masters of the Knights of Malta. The allées terminate in a terrace overlooking the Tiber and Janiculum. A staircase, now blocked off, leads down to the banks of the river.

Portrait bust in a rusti-cated wall niche

Following:
Flower-filled parterres in the spring

177 · *Villa of the Knights of Malta*

179 · *Villa of the Knights of Malta*

Villa Cimbrone

Ravello
Gardens open to the public all
year

The temple of Bacchus, with a statue by Gioacchino Varlese, houses the ashes of Lord Grimthorpe

Ravello is worth a pilgrimage. It is one of those places that remain with you always for its haunting loveliness. Pilgrimages imply a difficulty of arrival, and Ravello is no exception. Whether you brave the harrowing Neapolitan traffic, cross the mountains, or wend your way along the twisting coastline and then climb the snaking roads to the village of Ravello, the trip is not easy. The rewards are a beautiful pulpit in the Duomo and two nostalgic gardens with spectacular views, Villa Rufolo and Villa Cimbrone.

Villa Cimbrone is truly eclectic. It consciously borrows its cloistered architecture from Villa Rufolo. Hence there is a strong Medieval flavor, reinforced by the pseudo-Gothic villa, so dear to English taste at the turn of the nineteenth century. There are ancient Roman touches—perhaps partially influenced by nearby Villa Jovis on Capri. Fragments from excavations dot the garden: amphorae, columns, bits and pieces of sculpture. The garden is arranged to frame views of the Gulf of Salerno with belvederes and an unforgettable terrace, much as the ancient Romans constructed their seaside villas. Two parallel *viales*, or grand paths, cut through the garden to the tip of the spur of land, which juts out high above the sea. There is also a parallel stretch of lawn adjacent to the villa, which helps knit the garden together, considering the irregularity and piecemeal development of the site. The formal parterre gardens with their pavilions are placed off to the right of the main *viale*, reached by cross paths and steps. There is a large area that interweaves with the terrace continuing down the western slope through olive groves, which has a natural landscape flavor. The Temple of Bacchus here echoes the Temple of Venus at Hadrian's Villa; it is similarly perched on a precipice, with views of the rugged landscape beyond. Given the natural beauty of the zone, part of the delight of this garden is the incorporation of fields of wildflowers, the rocky terrain, the sunbaked scents, and the turquoise water alongside the formal garden features. This is not a Classical Italian garden in the rigid sense, although it contains elements of one.

The creation of Villa Cimbrone is the joint effort of two men, a romantic Englishman and his personal assitant. Ernest William

The belvedere of Mercury overlooking the sea

Beckett, later Lord Grimthorpe, was persuaded in 1904 to buy the property by Nicola Mansi, a native of Ravello. Mansi met Beckett in England, abandoned his trade as a tailor, and became Beckett's landscape architect and custodian of the villa. He supervised the transformation of an abandoned farm house over fifteen years. The garden was built in stages, which accounts for the lack of a unified plan. Mansi's father was a stone mason, and the gardens reflect this inherited interest in its cloisters, garden walls, and the terrace itself. Clipped green hedges occur only alongside the villa's lawn.

After traversing narrow twisting streets, passing the convents of San Francesco and Santa Chiara, one arrives on foot at an arched door. Immediately beyond on the left is the *chiostrino,* or little cloister, built in 1917 based on that of Villa Rufolo. Biforate arches lead off to the rooms of the villa and down to the so-called crypt. In the center of the *chiostrino* is a square well, with small spiral columns set in the corners. The arches of the crypt are also based on those found at Villa Rufolo. The crypt provides a lovely view of the sea from Maiori to Capo d'Orso and the steep hills beyond.

A wrought-iron gate sets off the private garden of the villa. This borders the eastern edge of the spur. A tall hedge of cypress ensures privacy from the main *viale,* which leads to the Temple of Ceres. Her statue stands within a pavilion set at a slight angle to the spectacular terrace built between 1911 and 1913. Its view is one of the most famed of Europe, overlooking the Amalfi coast to the waters of the Mediterranean three hundred feet below. Weathered marble busts ornament the slightly curving balcony. Benches with old cypresses behind them invite lingering.

From the terrace a second *viale* leads down a narrow, shaded way

The walled rose garden

to the *bosco* and the Belvedere of Mercury. The path meanders along the cliff to a short cypress allée ending at the Temple of Bacchus. This round temple with fluted doric columns encloses a bronze statue of a satyr with the young Bacchus by Gioacchino Varlese. This is the tomb of Lord Grimthorpe.

Nearby, the path passes the Grotto of Eve, although, strangely, a marble statue of Venus is seated inside. From here one traverses a wisteria arbor and a meadow where hortensia blooms in the summer. The path leads up to a walled rose garden, surrounded by a crumbling

wall set with tiles. Big pines grow around it. Snapdragons are mixed with varieties of roses in the formal, wedge-shaped beds.

Just beyond the rose garden is a tea loggia. This pavilion has Moorish arches inlaid with green and yellow tiles at the corners. Before the loggia stand four carved, antique columns from the ancient city of Paestum, bronze gazelles, and a fountain with figures of women. Off to the side are copies of Donatello's and Andrea del Verrocchio's statues of David. Flowerbeds are a riot of color, filled with yellow, white, and blue pansies, and miniature carnations.

183 · *Villa Cimbrone*

Palazzo Rufolo

Ravello
Gardens open to the public
June to September

A wisteria-covered well in a sheltered corner of Palazzo Rufolo

Palazzo Rufolo was a great source of inspiration for writers and musicians down through the centuries. Its importance to garden history lies in the unique preservation of a secular Medieval garden. Although cloister gardens have survived from the Middle Ages, no other lay garden from this period remains so intact in Italy.

In his *Decameron* (Day Two, Novella IV), Giovanni Boccaccio described the Amalfi coast as full of small cities, gardens, and fountains. Ravello in the fourteenth century was inhabited by merchants made wealthy by sea trade with the Near East. According to Boccaccio, the richest of these was Landolfo Rufolo. The Rufolo family flourished from the twelfth through the fourteenth centuries. Beginning with Giovanni in 1150 and ending with Pellegrino, who died in 1401, the Rufolos produced generations of Ravello bishops. In between, Nicola Rufolo commissioned the beautiful pulpit by Niccolò di Bartolomeo da Foggia found in the cathedral and planned the villa's garden. His son, Matteo, had banking dealings with King Charles I d'Anjou in nearby Naples. His royal crown was held as collateral for a Rufolo family loan in 1275.

The Confalone family inherited the villa from the Rufolos. In turn the Muscettola family held the property, and let it deteriorate until the eighteenth century, when the D'Afflittos reorganized the villa.

Among the distinguished visitors were King Charles II and his son Robert the Wise. The latter's illegitimate daughter, Maria d'Aquino, was the model for Fiammetta, Boccaccio's muse in *Visione Amorosa* (whom he meets for the first time in a garden). It has been suggested that Villa Rufolo was the inspiration for Boccaccio's setting of the *Decameron*, described as a mountaintop villa with a beautiful courtyard, loggias, and marvelous gardens with wells of very fresh water.

In a letter dated May 26, 1880, Richard Wagner after a visit to Villa Rufolo, exclaimed, "Finally I have found the enchanted garden of Klingsor!" In his last opera, *Parsifal*, a tower vanishes to reveal a tropical garden next to a magnificent castle. Parsifal, in his madness, is invited to play with flower maidens. The spell is broken when he catches the Holy Spear hurled at him by Klingsor; after making the sign of the cross with it, the castle disappears and the garden becomes a wilderness. The gardens of Villa Rufolo did become a wilderness over the centuries until purchased in 1851 by Francis Neville Reid. Under the guidance of the director of excavations at Pompeii, the gardens were restored, yet inevitably hints of nineteenth-century romantic tastes filtered in. Pines and cypresses were added, yet it is possible that some plants are descendents of the original ones. In 1974 the property came under the control of the Regione Campania.

The entrance to the grounds of Palazzo Rufolo is found through a small tower set on one side of the main piazza of Ravello. Passing through the arch, one walks down a cypress allée, cool in the hot southern sun. Originally, this was a grape arbor. It leads to a second larger tower, designed for defense of the villa. Passing through it, one comes to an exquisite courtyard with a strong Moorish flavor. On three sides is a double loggia (the third side was destroyed in a storm in 1713). The middle level is ornamented with delicate arabesque arches on marble columns. These arches and details of the towers recall Moorish architecture, reminding us of the close trade links southern Italy had with Arab countries many centuries ago. This courtyard is currently being restored. A stairway leads to the park, set

On the loggia of the dining area overlooking the sea

on a sloping irregular space. Toward the sea is a long loggia with a semicircular recess at the end. This was an open dining room in the thirteenth century, planned to enjoy the sea views and breezes. Pink geraniums flourish along its sides. The loggia has a belvedere with steps leading down to a formal rectangular parterre terrace. Flowerbeds center on a small, round fountain pool. Lavender, sweet peas, and pansies bloom here in the spring. Wisteria grows on the far wall, near the Medieval *stanza da bagno,* or bathing room, recessed in the sustaining wall. Within is a pool with splendid views of the adjacent garden and sea beyond. The rugged hillside descends to the villages of Minori and Maiori. Around the corner of this terrace, another smaller garden hugs the side of the villa. The presence of palms here is another Moorish touch.

Wagner's memory lives on at Palazzo Rufolo; every summer performances of his music are given on the terrace overlooking the sea.

Left:
The main parterre where annual Wagner concerts are held

Acknowledgments

This book is dedicated to my mother, Lennie Chatfield, who has steadfastly encouraged me in my Italian researches over many years and introduced me to the basic skills of gardening.

In Europe, I wish to thank my photographer Liberto for his enthusiasm and persistence; my friends Patrick McCrea and Roswitha Otto for their unfailing help with transportation, their hospitality and encouragement, and all those who opened their gardens to us, assisted with introductions, and shared information: Marco Magnifico, Elisa Sissa, Mother Suor Teresa Marini, Giulio Lensi Orlandi, Signor Suardi, Marchioness Beatrice Crivelli, Benedetta Origo Crea, Baron Fabio Sergardi, Lapo Mazzei, Count Alvise da Schio, Prince Alessandro Ruspoli, Santino Garbuglio, Marion de Jacobert, Jan Van Rossem, Alessandra and Azzurra Sommi-Picenardi, Count Briano Castelbarco-Albani, Count Clemente Castelbarco-Albani, Professor Pietro Terrosi Vagnoli, Marquis Emilio Pucci, Count Giannino Marzotto, Signor Firato of Locanda del'Sant'Uffizio, Maria Cicogna Farina, Margherita Sergardi, Marquises Luigi Brivio Sforza and Alessandro Brivio Sforza, Count Cesare and Countess Nicoletta Balduino, Domenico Fraccaroli, Paolo Peyron, Roberto Severi, Maria Cristina Mazzeschi, Signora Benedetti, Countess Marina Emo Capodilista, Guido Tommasi Aliotti, and Countess d'Entreves.

On this side of the Atlantic, I owe special thanks to my editor Sarah Burns for her skillful, patient work once again; to Fred Schwerin, who introduced me to Rizzoli, and enabled me to go off to Italy for months of research; and to Mother Jerome, O. S. B., for her memories and prayers.

Bibliography

Arntz, Wilhelm. "Villa Bettoni," *Garten Kunst*, 1910, 2:xii.

Acton, Sir Harold. *Great Houses of Italy: The Tuscan Villas*. New York: Viking Press, 1973.

Agnelli, Marella. *Gardens of the Italian Villas*. New York: Rizzoli International Publications, 1987.

Aillard, Charlotte. "The Ruspoli Legacy in Italy," *Architectural Digest*, July 1989.

Attlee, Helena, and Alex Ramsay. *Italian Gardens*. London: Robertson McCarta Ltd., 1989.

Bacciotti, Emilio. *Guida di Firenze*. Florence: 1886.

Baldinucci, Filippo. *Notizie dei professori del disegno (1767–1774)*. Florence: Eurografica, 1974.

Bascapè, Giacomo C. *Arte e storia dei giardini di Lombardia*. Milan: Cisalpino-La Goliardica, 1978.

Bassanese, Giuseppe Betussi. *Descrizione del Cataio Luogo del marchese Pio Enea degli Obizi . . . fatta da Giuseppe Betussi Bassanese l'anno MDLXXII con l'aggiunta del Co Francesco Berni delle fabriche, & altre delizie accresciutevi in 18 anni dal Marchese Pio Enea*. Ferrara, Italy: 1669.

Bedford, Rev. W. K. R. *Malta and the Knights Hospitallers*. London: 1894.

Le Blond, Mrs. Aubrey. *The Old Gardens of Italy*. London: 1926.

Boccardi, Renzo. "Villa di San Remigio," *Emporium*, 1913.

Boriosi, Maria Cruciani. "I Giardini dell'Italia centro-settentrionale di derivazione tosco-romana," in *Antichità Viva*, volume 3. Florence: Edam, 1970.

Borsi, Franco, and Geno Pampaloni. *Ville e giardini*. Novara, Italy: Istituto Geografico de Agostini, 1984.

Brenna, Gian Giuseppe. *Tremezzina*. Como, Italy: Cairoli, 1969.

Bruni, Bruno. *Un Giardino all'Italiana a Pesaro*, volume 13. Pesaro, Italy: Esercitazioni della Accademia Agraria di Pesaro, 1981.

Camerieri, Paolo, Daniel and Giuseppe Corbucci, and Giuseppe Donati. *Provincia di Perugia collezione Maria Teresa Straka Coppa e Francesco Coppa—*

Villa Fidele. Perugia, Italy: Amministrazione provinciale di Perugia, 1988.

Cevese, Renato. *Ville della provincia di Vicenza*. Milan: Sisar, 1980.

Cresti, Carlo. *Itinerari della città degli Uffizi*. Florence: Bonechi, 1982.

Dal Re, Marcantonio. *Le Delizie della villa di Castellazzo*. 1742.

———. *Ville di delizia*. 1726. Reprint. Milan: Polifilo, 1963.

Dami, Luigi. *The Italian Garden*. New York: Brentano, 1925.

De Brosses, Charles. *Le Président De Brosses en Italie: Lettres familières écrites d'Italie en 1739 et 1740*. Paris: 1858.

Dickens, Charles. *Pictures from Italy*. Geneva, Switzerland: Edito Serice, 1844.

Elgood, George S. *Italian Gardens*. London: Longmans, Green, 1907.

Faccini, Mario. *Guida ai giardini d'Italia*. Milan: Ottaviano, 1983.

Fariello, Francesco. *Architettura dei giardini*. Rome: Scipioni Editore and Edizioni dell'Ateneo. 1985.

Fiorani, Camillo. *Giardini d'Italia*. Rome: Mediterranée, 1960.

Franck, Carl L. *The Villas of Frascati*. New York: Transatlantic Arts; London: Alec Tiranti Ltd., 1966 (Co-editions).

Goode, Patrick, Geoffrey and Susan Jellicoe, and Michael Lancaster. *The Oxford Companion to Gardens*. New York: Oxford University Press, 1987.

Grant, Michael. *Cities of Vesuvius—Pompeii and Herculaneum*. Harmondsworth, England: Penguin, 1976.

Gromort, Georges. *Jardins d'Italie*. Paris: A. Vincent, 1902.

Guida dell'Orto Botanico. Padua, Italy: Università degli Studi di Padova, 1986.

Guida d'Italia: Firenze e dintorni. Milan: Touring Club, 1974.

Hare, Christopher. *The Most Illustrious Ladies of the Italian Renaissance*. New York: Charles Scribner's Sons, 1905.

Horner, Susan and Joanna. *Walks in Florence and its Environs*, volume 1. London: 1884.

Langé, Santino. *Ville italiane: Lombardia*. Milan: Rusconi Immagine, 1984.

———. *Ville della provincia di Milano*. Milan: Edizioni Sisar, 1972.

Latham, Charles, and E. March Phillipps. *The Gardens of Italy*. London: Country Life Ltd., 1905.

Lensi Orlandi, Giulio. *Le Ville di Firenze*. 1954. Reprint. Florence: Vallecchi, 1978.

Lumachi, Francesco. *Firenze e dintorni*. Florence: 1928.

McGuire, Frances Margaret. *Gardens of Italy*. London: Heinemann, 1964.

Mader, Gunter, and Laila G. Neubert-Mader. *Giardini all'italiana*. Milan: Rizzoli, 1987.

Maiuri, Amedeo. *Pompeii*. Rome: La Libreria Dello Stato, 1949.

———. *Pompeii*. Novara, Italy: Istituto de Agostini, 1956.

Mancini, Gioacchino. *Villa Adriana e Villa d'Este*. Rome: La Libreria dello Stato, 1969.

Masson, Georgina. *Italian Gardens*. New York: Harry N. Abrams, 1961.

Mazzeschi, Maria Cristina, and Roberto Severi. *Il Giardino storico della villa 'il Campaccio' nella Val d'Esse di Cortona*." Florence: University of Florence, 1989.

Morrell, Lady Ottoline. *Memoirs of Lady Ottoline Morrell, A Study in Friendship 1873–1915*, ed. Robert Gathorne Hardy. New York: Knopf, 1964.

Mulhern, Alice. *Basilica of SS Quattro Coronati*. Rome: Augustinian Sisters of SS. Quattro Coronati, n.d.

Muraro, Michelangelo. *Venetian Villas*. Udine, Italy: Magnus, 1986.

Nichols, Rose Standish. *Italian Pleasure Gardens*. New York: Dodd Mead & Company, 1928.

Nobile, Bianca Marta. *I Giardini d'Italia*. Bologna, Italy: Calderini, 1984.

Origo, Iris. *Images and Shadows, Part of a Life*. New York: Harcourt Brace & Jovanovich, 1970.

Perogalli, Carlo, and Maria Grazia Sandri. *Ville delle province di Bergamo e Brescia*. Milan: Edizioni Sisar, 1969.

Romby, Giuseppina, and Renato Stopani. *I Giardini del Chianti*. Florence: Centro di Studi Storici Chiantigiani, 1989.

Ross, Janet. *Florentine Villas*. London: Dent & Co., 1901.

Sassoli, Mario Gori. *La villa Venuti di Catrosse a Cortona notizie e documenti/ Accademia Etrusca di Cortona*. Cortona, Italy: Calosci, 1984.

Shepherd, J. C., and G. A. Jellicoe. *Italian Gardens of the Renaissance*. New York: Charles Scribner's Sons, 1925.

Tabarelli, Gian Maria. *Castelli dell'Alto Adige*. Milan: Görlich, 1974.

Tagliolini, Alessandro. *I Giardini di Roma*. Rome: Newton Compton, 1980.

———. *Storia del giardino italiano*. Florence: La Casa Usher, 1988.

Talia, Marzi Cocozza, Vittorio Marzi, Antonio Ventrelli, and Damiano Ventrelli. *Giardini d'arte*. Bologna, Italy: Edagricole, 1986.

Torselli, Giorgio. *Ville di Roma*. Rome: Compagnia Edizioni Internazionali, 1968.

Triggs, H. Inigo. *The Art of Garden Design in Italy*. London: Longmans, Green, 1906.

Vasari, Giorgio. *The Lives of the Painters, Sculptors and Architects*, trans. A. B. Hinds. London: Dent & Co., 1963.

Visentini, Margherita Azzi. *Il Giardino Veneto*. Milan: Electa, 1988.

Viviani, Giuseppe Franco, ed. *La Villa nel veronese*. Verona, Italy: Banca Mutua Popolare di Verona, 1975.

Walker, John, and Amery Aldrich. *A Guide to Villas and Gardens in Italy for the American Academy in Rome*. Florence: 1938.

Watson, Derek. *Richard Wagner, A Biography*. New York: Schirmer Books, 1979.

Westernhagen, Curt von. *Wagner, A Biography*, volume 2. Cambridge, England: Cambridge University Press, 1978.

Wharton, Edith. *Italian Villas & Their Gardens*. Reprint. New York: Da Capo, 1976.

Wright, Richardson. *The Story of Gardening*. 1934. Reprint. New York: Dover Publications, 1963.

Index

PHOTOGRAPHY CREDITS